The Mine & the Mint

The Mine & the Mint

SOURCES FOR THE WRITINGS OF

Thomas De Quincey

ALBERT GOLDMAN

Southern Illinois University Press

CARBONDALE AND EDWARDSVILLE

For Florence

ACKNOWLEDGMENTS

It is a pleasure to acknowledge my indebtedness to those who aided in the design and execution of this study. Particularly, I wish to thank Professor Jerome Buckley, who offered many valuable criticisms of the text and suggested the general plan of organization. Professor Marshall Suther was most helpful in suggesting stylistic improvements. Dr. Thomas I. Rae, Assistant Keeper of the National Library of Scotland, compiled for my use a list of the De Quincey manuscripts held by the Library and arranged for the microfilming of the *Blackwood's Magazine* MSS. Miss Dorothea R. Wesel, Assistant Librarian of Hunter College, and Mr. John Sherman aided me in obtaining rare books, particularly from the Yale University Library and the Newberry Library, whose librarians likewise I wish to thank. I am obliged to Miss Marlene Fisher and Mr. Paul Proskauer, former colleagues at Hunter College, for verifying my translations of French and German passages and to Joseph Epstein for editorial assistance. By far my greatest debt is to Florence Goldman, without whose aid, advice and encouragement this book could not have been written.

CONTENTS

The Mine & the Mint

"For the fact is, that the labourers of the Mine
(as I am accustomed to call them), or those who
dig up the metal of truth, are seldom fitted to
be also labourers of the Mint—i.e. to work up
the metal for current use."

I

The Background

THE TRADITIONAL VIEW of Thomas De Quincey as a poly-histor, or universal authority on matters of scholarly and intellectual interest, has been acknowledged and reaffirmed by almost every student of his life and writings from the late nineteenth century down to the present day. The first critic fully to elaborate this view was David Masson, the author of *Thomas De Quincey*, the biography in the English Men of Letters Series, and the editor of the standard edition of his works, *The Collected Writings of Thomas De Quincey*. As Professor Masson's presentation is the most thorough, sympathetic and emphatic of all the many discussions of this subject, it deserves to be quoted at length. After commenting on the extreme multifariousness of De Quincey's writings, Masson concludes:

> His main interest in life was that of universal curiosity, sheer inquisitiveness and meditativeness about all things whatsoever. Hence his early passion for the acquisition of book-knowledge, and the fact that before his twenty-fifth year he had read so much and so variously as to be even more entitled to the name of polyhistor than almost any of his English contemporaries . . . add moreover a preter-naturally tenacious memory; and it will be seen with what an unusual stock of materials De Quincey came to the craft of magazine authorship. When he did so in his thirty-fifth year, it was under the compulsion of circumstances. He would rather not have adopted the craft; he

would rather have gone on still as a private student and observer, with the chance of some outcome in laboured book-form at his own leisure; but, once harnessed to the periodical printing-press, he was at no loss for matter. His command of German greatly increased in those days his range into the unhackneyed and uncommon; but, without that help, his extensive readings in the classics, in medieval Latin, and in our earlier and less-known English authors, would have sufficed, in the grasp of a memory so retentive as his, to impart to his writings much of that polyhistoric character, that multifariousness of out-of-the-way learning, which we discern in them.

. . . .

At the basis of all, as we have seen, was his learning, his wealth of miscellaneous and accurate knowledge. . . . Whatever else De Quincey was, he was at all events a scholar and polyhistor.[1]

The traditional estimate of Thomas De Quincey rests upon a very extensive body of evidence consisting not only of De Quincey's numerous works of scholarship, but also of the statements of his friends and acquaintances, the records of his conversation, and his own self-critical observations. De Quincey was an extremely self-conscious man, and his various autobiographical writings provide a complete and finely detailed self-portrait. In his first and most famous composition, *The Confessions of an English Opium Eater*, a work bearing the significant sub-title, "An Extract from the Life of a Scholar," De Quincey defines himself in these terms: "For my own part, without breach of truth or modesty, I may affirm, that my life has been, on the whole, the life of a philosopher: from my birth, I was made an intellectual creature; and intellectual in the highest sense my pursuits and pleasures have been, even from my school-boy days."[2]

Even these "school-boy days," he relates in another passage from the *Confessions*, were distinguished by extraordinary classical attainments:

I was sent to various schools, great and small; and was very early distinguished for my classical attainments, especially for my knowledge of Greek. At thirteen I wrote Greek with ease; and at fifteen my command of that language was so great, that I not only composed Greek verses in lyric metres, but would converse in Greek fluently, and without embarrassment—an accomplishment which I have not since met with in any scholar of my times, and which, in my case, was owing to the practice of daily reading off the newspapers into the best Greek I could furnish extempore.[3]

The evidence of De Quincey's vast reading throughout the course of his life is so profuse that one can content himself with a single statement taken from his paper on Coleridge: "I will assert finally that, . . . [I have] read for thirty years in the same track as Coleridge—that track in which few of any age will ever follow us, such as German metaphysicians, Latin schoolmen, thaumaturgic Platonists, religious Mystics." (II, 147)

There does not appear to be any exaggeration in these complacent self-appraisals, for a number of reports of De Quincey's conversation are unanimous in their illustration of enormous erudition fully assimilated and splendidly displayed. There is, for example, the well-known passage in which Robert Pearse Gillies, the friend of De Quincey's early years, describes the soaring flight and exalted range of his conversation:

The talk might be of "beeves," and he could grapple with them if expected to do so, but his musical cadences were not in keeping with such work, and in a few minutes (not without some strictly logical sequence) he could escape at will from beeves to butterflies, and thence to the soul's immortality, to Plato, and Kant, and Schelling, and Fichte, to Milton's early years and Shakespeare's sonnets, to Wordsworth and Coleridge, to Homer and Eschylus, to St. Thomas of Aquin, St. Basil, and St. Chrysostom.[4]

A more sober and detailed account is found in Richard Woodhouse's "Notes of Conversations with Thomas De Quincey." Woodhouse met De Quincey at the time of the first publication of the *Confessions* and, anticipating great things from so glamorous a figure as the English Opium Eater, he was not disappointed, as the following report indicates:

> The Opium Eater appears to have read a great deal, and to have thought much more. I was astonished at the depth and *reality*, if I may so call it, of his knowledge. He seems to have passed nothing that occurred in the course of his study unreflected on or unremembered. His conversation appeared like the elaboration of a mine of results: and if at any time a general observation of his became matter of question or ulterior disquisition it was found that he had ready his reasons at a moment's notice; so that it was clear that his opinions were the fruits of his own reflections on what had come before him, and had not been taken up from others. Indeed, this last clearly appeared, since upon most of the topics that arose he was able to give a very satisfactory account, not merely of *what books* had been written upon those subjects, but of *what opinions* had been entertained upon them, together with his own judgments of those opinions, his acquiescence in them, or qualifications in them. Upon almost every subject that was introduced he had not only that general information which is easily picked up in literary society or from books, but that minute and accurate acquaintance with the details that can be acquired only from personal investigation of a subject and reflection upon it at the same time. Taylor led him into political economy, into the Greek and Latin accents, into antiquities, Roman roads, old castles, the origin and analogy of languages; upon all these he was informed to considerable minuteness. The same with regard to Shakespeare's sonnets, Spenser's minor poems, and the great writers and characters of Elizabeth's age and those of Cromwell's time. His judgments of books, of writers, of politics, were particularly satisfactory and sound.[5]

Such a statement is both impressive and suggestive. But it is upon the abundant evidence supplied by De Quincey's published writings, especially those of a scholarly nature, that the traditional view of him as a polyhistor fundamentally rests. As a scholar, De Quincey appears to have been unique in the extraordinary breadth of his learning and in his preference for difficult and esoteric themes. His range extended from the ancient to the modern literatures, from metaphysics to political economy, from the history of great national epochs and events to the private lives of famous men. His penchant for the remote and recondite is suggested by such titles on his own works as "The Essenes," "Toilette of the Hebrew Lady," "The Casuistry of Roman Meals," "Historico-Critical Inquiry into the origin of the Rosicrucians and the Free-masons." Measured merely by their number, De Quincey's scholarly writings constitute an impressive achievement. In his classical studies alone, the following titles appear: "Homer and the Homeridae," "The Philosophy of Herodotus," "The Theban Sphinx," "The Pagan Oracles," "Plato's Republic," "A Brief Appraisal of the Greek Literature in its Foremost Pretensions," "Theory of Greek Tragedy," "The Philosophy of Roman History," "Cicero," and "The Caesars."

While these are academic themes, it was not as an academic scholar that De Quincey fancied himself. Rather, he believed his role was that of the bold and original thinker posing traditional problems in a new light and offering novel and paradoxical solutions. He is quite explicit about his intention to present only original ideas:

> to think reasonably upon any question, has never been allowed by me as a sufficient ground for writing upon it, unless I believed myself able to offer some considerable novelty.

(1, 14)

With such an overwhelming body of evidence to support his pretensions to scholarly erudition and intellectual sophistication, it is not to be thought that modern criticism would seriously challenge De Quincey's right to his time-honored title of polyhistor. And, in fact, almost every modern student of De Quincey has paid his respects to him as a man of learning; however, one does detect in most modern treatments of him a certain discomfort and embarrassment, for modern scholars are very much aware of the fact that De Quincey, who wrote almost all of his pieces for publication in popular literary magazines, was not above the unscholarly practices of the literary journalist. His works abound in exaggerations, forced emphases, bizarre points of view, and all the other stimulants that the journalist uses to whet the common reader's curiosity.[6] Inevitably, in an age of scientific scholarship, the antiquated technique of De Quincey's investigations has called forth criticism which stresses the inadequacy of his research and the frequent unsoundness of his conclusions. The modern view of De Quincey is decidedly ambivalent, but the consensus seems to be that he was a learned man writing down to a popular audience and, therefore, careless of that accuracy of statement and balance of judgment which are the ideals of a genuine scholar.

The current attitude has been forcibly expressed by Professor Oliver Elton: "[De Quincey] is the Renaissance type of *polyhistor*, or man of universal information, driven to become a modern pressman for bread; the best-equipped, perhaps, of all the Englishmen then living who fell to such an industry."[7] Professor Eaton, the author of the standard life, *Thomas De Quincey: A Biography*, has much the same idea, though his tone is more moderate. "Fundamentally, De Quincey with all his learning was hardly a scholar in the full modern sense; at least, his opportunities for exhaustive research were not used. His mind was encyclopedic; his sympathies were philosophic; but his concern was with popularizing."[8]

In general, then, the modern view of De Quincey's intellectual character would appear to be substantially the same as that entertained by the critics of the nineteenth century, and this even though his works do not command today the respect once accorded them.

This being the case, it cannot help but cause present-day scholars to reform rather drastically their notion of De Quincey when they learn, as the following discussion will demonstrate, that his many works of a scholarly or intellectual nature are almost all derived in the most direct way from printed sources, and in almost every case from a single volume. In every article of this kind, De Quincey has produced a clever piece of hack work, writing with the source book in one hand and the pen in the other—translating, abstracting, and abridging, piecing together inadequate notes preserved for such purposes, and in general working like some hard-pressed inhabitant of Grub Street.

In some cases what De Quincey has done must simply be regarded as plagiarism of the most flagrant sort, in which the writer deliberately affixes his name to another man's work. But usually he is not guilty of such crude malpractice. Generally he endeavored, according to his abilities, to appropriate the materials with which he worked, at least to the extent of rearranging them and improving their language. The details of his practice will be fully described in the succeeding pages, though here it should be pointed out that it is not the intention of this study simply to demolish De Quincey's pretensions, and with them his reputation as a serious and important figure in nineteenth century English literature. Indeed, while the study of De Quincey's writings in relation to their sources decisively diminishes his scholarly pretensions, at the same time such a study also tends to enhance his literary reputation by revealing fresh evidence of his capacities as an *imaginative* writer. In some instances—and these from the literary point of view are perhaps the most important ones —he has added so much of his own invention to the source material that he could have legitimately claimed the final product as original imaginative composition, had he not always the compulsion to pass it off as scholarship.

For it is one of the peculiar traits of De Quincey's character that he must invariably work as though behind a mask; and even when he has expended the most enormous efforts in recasting some wretched piece of historiography or biography, he must perforce claim that his original and highly imaginative work is an authentic and scholarly document. This strange and perverse passion for truth—or at least for an appearance of truthfulness—can be ascribed, as will be shown, either to his practical sense that a romanticized version of historical fact would not be acceptable to his English readers, or else to some deep peculiarity in his nature which made the act of creation something secret and furtive, something that must never be openly avowed.

However this may be, it is the central fact of De Quincey's literary career that when, as was so often the case, he could not simply write out of his own experience and his own fantasy-like imaginings, he fell back upon the arts of the hack journalist. Yet when he did so, it was not that he was hurried or indifferent to the literary proprieties, but that these dubious practices enabled him at least to write, and for him, writing was, in more than one sense of the word, life. It is, then, with this new sense of De Quincey as a writer for long periods of time utterly dependent upon the opportunities afforded him by the wind-blown chances of casual reading and casual investigation that this study is concerned. And, as will become clear, through most of his years it was by reworking literary source materials that De Quincey survived as an author.

This view of De Quincey as a writer profoundly dependent upon external sources of information and opinion is not one that should so long have remained obscure.[9] Strangely enough, the primary evidence for it lies quite openly upon the surface of De Quincey's work itself. In paper after paper, he states if the reader will but attend to him, that what he is writing has in fact been derived from some other source. Frequently, in the introduction to an article or paper, he will assert that he has drawn his facts from an author or a book that he refers to by name or title. Thus, in the introduction to his delightful account of the last days of Immanuel Kant, he cites three German authorities for the facts upon which his narrative is based. His elaborate description of the toilet of a Hebrew lady is, he openly states, his digest of a cumbersome work by a German scholar. Some of his informative or didactic papers are cast in the form of book reviews, and the reader is made aware that the author is drawing upon the book under review for information, although the opinions he expresses are presumably original. "Richard Bentley," his life of the great English classicist, is a pre-eminent example of De Quincey's practice of writing extensive expositions on occasions offered by book reviews.

And then there are several instances in his later years of De Quincey's revealing, either in some subsequent publication or in the notes prepared for his collected edition,[10] the sources of articles or papers which, upon their first publication, appeared to rise solely from his own store of knowledge. When it first appeared, the famous account of the flight of a Tartar tribe contained no indication of its true source in the publication of a German traveler; but in an article written during his last years, De Quincey alludes to this German traveler and his book, thereby making it possible to trace his source. Sometimes these later indications of borrowings have the character of a confession or even an apology. Thus, De Quincey is found owning up to the plagiarism he committed twenty-three years before, in this instance upon a German professor's book on the Rosicrucians and Freemasons, in these self-defensive terms:

> It was a paper in this sense mine, that from me it had received form and arrangement; but the materials belonged to the learned German—viz. Buhle. . . . No German has any conception of style. I therefore did him the favour to wash his dirty face, and make him presentable amongst Christians; but the substance was drawn entirely from this German book.
>
> (VII, 201–2)

The amount of scholarly comment which has been prompted by these patent indications of indebtedness to literary source materials is remarkably small. Aside from a few allusions scattered about in biographies or studies of various kinds (most of them erroneous) and two dissertations of very narrow scope,[11] until now the principal source of information on the subject of De Quincey's borrowings has been the disquisitions found in the *apparatus criticus* of David Masson's standard edition of De Quincey's writings. From the opportunity presented of reviewing the writer's entire production while compiling his edition, Masson was able to piece together a number of allusions to sources, and from these hints to track down the actual source materials for several important papers. But, in view of the abundance of suggestions for source studies which De Quincey's writings contain, the limited extent of Masson's comments indicates that he, too, had failed to grasp the principle behind De Quincey's practice; and even in those few instances in which Masson does compare a work of De Quincey's with its source, the treatment is slight or summary, a note or an appendix. Furthermore, there is a tendency on Masson's part to minimize the degree of De Quincey's indebtedness even where it is most obvious, thus making a case for his author's originality.

The example of Masson is instructive, for it indicates

why this whole question has so long been ignored. There are, in fact, several reasons: for one, there is the appearance of ingenuousness that De Quincey puts on in citing his sources. When an author states that his work is merely a digest of several other authors, the reader is not likely to suspect that it is actually a translation of one. For another, when one reads a superbly written biographical sketch of some forty or fifty pages, he is not likely to think that this elaborate and polished composition is simply an abstract of a book written in English and readily available to the author's readers. And then, of course, there is a tendency to assume that writings that attain a high degree of stylistic originality must be wholly original writings. Translations generally bear the imprint of the style of the original. Thus, what with the prevalent over-charitable assumptions about De Quincey, who is after all a classic of his literature, and the difficulty in evading the snares he has artfully laid in the reader's path, the whole extent and degree of his plagiarisms and related practices has been overlooked. But once one begins to read De Quincey with one's eyes open to the possibility that his writings are directly derived from printed sources, indications of such sources are to be found everywhere. Even among his personal reminiscences there are papers, presumably based on his own experience, that prove to be artful reworkings of accounts which he received at second hand from books and other printed documents.

This heavy reliance upon printed source material is characteristic of De Quincey's entire literary career, and it may be said in general that it formed his usual method of writing when, as was often the case, he could not find his way back to those early experiences and secret fantasies that inspired the *Confessions*, the "Suspiria," and his other purely original writings. However, the findings of this study are suggestive even for these wholly original writings, for there is no reason to doubt that the same

imaginative processes that characterize De Quincey's rewriting of his sources were also applied to that other and
greater "source"—the writer's own experience. And here
can be seen the importance of all those doubts and suspicions, voiced from the time of the first publication of the
Confessions, about the veracity of De Quincey's record of
his own experience and his reports of the doings of those
famous men, Wordsworth, Coleridge, Lamb, and others,
with whom he long consorted—doubts that now appear
substantiated by the sense one gains of De Quincey's inveterate tendency to recast and reimagine everything that
excited his interest.[12]

That sophisticated view of De Quincey which makes
him out to be essentially an imaginative author, a writer
of romance, here finds its strongest confirmation, for there
is now good reason to believe that every subject he touched
he transformed in much the same way. It is, after all, but
a difference of degree to distinguish in a case like De
Quincey's between original writings and those based on
literary sources, when the process that transforms the
printed source material is probably the same process that
has made the raw stuff of experience into literature. The
transforming imagination of the writer is always the same.
Its tendency is not essentially altered by its point of departure. If there existed a journal or diary of De Quincey's
dreams, his adventures, a record in the form of a hastily
noted memoir of his first meeting with Wordsworth or
Coleridge, his conversations with Lamb, or his immediate
sense of the English Lake Country, one would undoubtedly discover exactly the same differences between fact and
fancy as one finds in comparing the journal, memoir, or
treatise of some obscure German author with De Quincey's
revision of the same.

Therefore, this study is more concerned with the imaginative temperament of an author than with the sleights,
cheats, and hoaxes of a clever but unscrupulous journalist.

And it is accordingly essential to relate the peculiar practices by which De Quincey produced so many of his works to the character of his development as an imaginative being and as a man. Thus, before an analysis of De Quincey's writings in relation to his sources, it is perhaps best to sketch, in a summary fashion, the course of his early development: to draw him as he was when he embarked upon his long career of forty years, and to elucidate those circumstances in his life that particularly fostered his characteristic approach to writing.

2

De Quincey's literary aspirations, arising quite naturally out of a childhood spent in an intense absorption in reading and day-dreaming, manifested themselves at an early age.[13] When he was thirteen, he composed a tragedy on an historical subject;[14] at fifteen, he won a prize in a national competition for the best translation by a school-boy of an ode by Horace. (xiv, 368–69) About this time, in 1799, he read the *Lyrical Ballads,* an experience he later described as "the greatest event in the unfolding of my mind." (ii, 138) De Quincey's poetic ambitions gradually coalesced with his youthful admiration for Wordsworth, and he formed the bold resolution of running away from the Grammar School at Manchester to visit the Lake Country. (iii, 281) But what began as a daring bid for freedom and maturity became first a mere walking tour of Wales, and finally a dreadful ordeal of solitude and despair in London.

It is from the period immediately following his ignominious return home, that posterity has the deepest insight into the mind and character of the young De Quincey. A diary, written in 1803 during his seventeenth year, reveals him as a very sad, serious, and self-conscious young man.

He was constantly occupied in reading contemporary literature, most of it Gothic romances, formulating theories of
literary effects, and planning various literary projects.[15] "I
. . . always intended . . . poems should form the corner-
stones of my fame,"[16] he confides to his diary, and one may
be sure that he is thinking of Wordsworth and the *Lyrical
Ballads*. But the tales and poems and tragedies he mentions
are merely figments of an ambitious mind bent on literary
fame; there is no indication that he was actually engaged
in writing. Instead, he satisfied himself by beginning a
correspondence with Wordsworth, which elicited kind and
helpful replies and a most generous offer of friendship.[17]

The timidity with which De Quincey anticipated a meeting with the great poet was so intense that it was not until
1807, four years after his first correspondence with Wordsworth, that he finally met him in the Lake District. (II,
229–52) Meanwhile, in 1803, De Quincey had entered
Oxford and immersed himself in studies that consumed
five years of his life, but apparently did not tend to any
definite purpose; when he was to come up for his examinations, he felt himself ill-prepared, and upon a shallow pretext fled the college the day before the final test.[18]

In his first two years of residence at the University, he
spoke less than a hundred words (II, 61); yet he was fur-
nishing his mind with a great variety of information on
every sort of scholarly or academic subject. During these
years he had mastered the German language, had read
Kant, and had ventured forth—one of the first Englishmen
to do so—upon the vast ocean of German scholarship.
(II, 81–109)[19] During these college years, too, he had come
of age and received his patrimony, somewhat diminished
by debts he had incurred earlier and further reduced by
a generous but imprudent gift of three hundred pounds to
Coleridge.

The most important effect of these years, though, was
the final crystallization of his character, which is best seen

in the notion of the ideal life he formulated at this time and subsequently put into practice. His ideal was to retire to a comfortable home in some picturesque region, and there to devote himself to the cultivation of his mind and the exercise of his exquisite sensibilities. (II, 108 f) In 1809, soon after leaving Oxford, he realized this dream by taking up residence in the Lake District in Wordsworth's former home, Dove Cottage, where in comfortable circumstances he enjoyed his library of five thousand volumes, entertained the local *literati*, and contemplated nature. A famous passage in the *Confessions* epitomizes De Quincey's life in this period. With great gusto, he paints himself cozily ensconced in his cottage parlor beside a warm fire, holding in his hand a volume of Kant, while at his elbow stands a decanter of purple laudanum. (III, 409–10) He had long since become addicted to opium, having first tried its powers while a student at Oxford and having subsequently adjusted his life to the cyclical rhythm of intoxication and disintoxication. (III, 380)

There can be no question that his addiction strengthened the passive, dreamy tendency of his existence and provided, by the release it afforded to his extraordinary powers of fantasy, a satisfactory substitute for the real activity of creative writing and thinking. Conversation, too, which De Quincey cultivated increasingly as an art, further served to drain off his creative energies and to provide an alternative for literary expression. (X, 264–88) Had his financial resources been sufficient, it appears almost certain that he would have lived out his life in this manner and never have produced, or at least published, anything of consequence.[20]

As a disciple of Wordsworth, De Quincey was impelled to some slight literary activity; if for no other reason than by his desire to serve the purposes of the poet. Thus, as part of his work in seeing Wordsworth's pamphlet on the Convention of Cintra[21] through the press, he wrote to order a note of some pages in length concerning the letters of Sir John Moore, which was appended to the pamphlet. However, even such a small exertion he found taxing, and when later he was asked by the Wordsworths to write an answer to the critics of Wordsworth's poetry, he failed, after many promises, to perform the task.[22]

Even during his bachelor years at Dove Cottage, 1809 to 1816, De Quincey was disturbed by the thought of his dwindling capital. But his efforts to improve his position were characteristically fanciful and futile. Ruling out the possibility of turning a "trading author," he duped himself into thinking that he might, with a little effort, qualify himself as a lawyer, and after a relatively short period of lucrative practice, retire to his picturesque abode, once again financially sound. He even went so far as to enroll himself in Lincoln's Inn, and he may have kept a term or two, but clearly the intention was never seriously held.[23] Equally fanciful, it may be assumed, was his project of a great philosophical treatise to be entitled (after Spinoza) *De Emendatione Humani Intellectus*. (III, 431) De Quincey's intellectual ambitions were of that extreme order that makes any effort to realize them seem futile—a very convenient state of mind for one who is both idle and proud. Writing to his mother in 1818, he unfolds his fantasy at length.

> my ambition was—that, by long and painful labour combining with such faculties as God had given me, I might become the intellectual benefactor of my species. I hoped and have every year hoped with better grounds that, (if I should be blessed with life sufficient) I should accomplish a great revolution in the intellectual condition of the world; that I should both as one cause and as one effect of that revolution place education upon a new footing, throughout all civilized nations, was but one part of this revolution: it was also but a part (though

*it may seem singly more than enough for a whole) to
be the first founder of true Philosophy.*[24]

After nine years of living comfortably without a voca-
tion, disaster struck—and with triple force. First, he al-
ienated his dearest friends, the Wordsworths, by becoming
involved with the daughter of one of the Dalesmen. This
girl, Margaret Sympson, he married in 1817, but only after
their son had been born. Then, after a brief year of domestic joy, he suffered a nervous breakdown accompanied
by the most alarming symptoms of drug addiction—hallu-
cinations, apathy, and despondency. (III, 431–49) Recov-
ering at last from this debilitating illness, he found himself
practically destitute. His financial affairs were hopelessly
entangled, and the burden of his responsibilities was
steadily increasing. At this point, he rallied with the desperate energy of a man suddenly awakened to the dangers
of his position.

He conciliated Wordsworth by contributing a political
pamphlet to the cause of the Lowthers, Wordsworth's
patrons.[25] In return, Wordsworth used his influence to
obtain for De Quincey, in July 1818, the position of editor
of *The Westmoreland Gazette*. With no previous experience as a journalist, with the serious handicap of his passive and impractical nature, and with the lingering effects
of his illness still upon him, he made a bad job of the
editorship. After a little more than a year, he was forced
to resign. But the stimulus of his responsibilities had
forced his mind to work along practical lines, and during
his editorship he evolved the idea of a literary and philosophical gazette which, according to his editorial proposal,
would include contributions of four kinds: statistical tables, British and continental; original essays; a Horolegium
of unknown, inaccessible or neglected literature, chiefly
English; and translations of German literature and philosophy. The Horolegium, he wrote, would "admit none but

such articles as appear to come under these two conditions; first, that they shall be of extraordinary interest; secondly, that they shall from their situation appear to be of little notoriety. The second condition will not be thought realized, unless the article proposed for admission shall stand either first in a book of very ancient date, or secondly in a modern book of unusually high price, or thirdly, in a book of vast extent . . . ; or fourthly, in a book which from its general subject appears to have been very little read—or which appears, from having never reached a second edition (whether otherwise fitted or not for popularity), to have been in fact but little read."[26] But his journal's major claim to "originality and depth of interest" was to be its translations from German literature, "the most opulent in Europe."

> It is a perfect Potosi: and the English nation have as yet imported nothing but the coarsest part of the ore
>
> .   .   .   .
>
> It is in this department of intellectual power, in various branches of science, in historical documents and archives, and universally in all inquiries which demand very patient and elaborate research that Germany is eminent— and eminent above all competition from either ancient or modern times. It is from these departments of German literature that the Editor will draw his materials.[27]

De Quincey did not actually carry out these projects in the pages of *The Westmoreland Gazette*; but he worked at some of them, and in later years made use of his materials. More interesting, however, is the general nature of his projects, for it was precisely work of this sort that later formed the mainstay of his journalistic career.

But before his final commitment to journalism, there was yet another period: some two years of procrastination and delay during which his good friend, John Wilson (Christopher North) prevailed upon him to become a contributor to *Blackwood's Edinburgh Magazine*, a publication of which he, North, had become the editor. This time De Quincey went so far as to take up residence in Edinburgh in December, 1820, and start work on some articles for the magazine; but flushed with an unnatural sense of self-importance, he sent an unfortunate letter to Blackwood disparaging the quality of the magazine and humorously suggesting that he would have to be its main support, that he would be "the Atlas of the magazine."[28] After an angry exchange with the choleric Blackwood, the association was broken and De Quincey was not to appear in print until late in the following year when, having journeyed up to London, he made an arrangement with the proprietors of *The London Magazine* (assisted this time by Charles Lamb) to publish *The Confessions of an English Opium Eater*, which was serialized in the magazine in the months of September and October, 1821.

The enormous acclaim that the anonymous author of the *Confessions* received from the reading public made De Quincey's position as a journalist secure forever. With one stroke he had established himself as the leading literary journalist of his day, easily surpassing in fame—or at least in notoriety—Charles Lamb, William Hazlitt, and Thomas Hood, his fellow contributors to *The London Magazine*.[29] But in a single contribution for which he had been paid a mere forty pounds, he had exhausted his best vein. A promised third installment of the *Confessions* never appeared, and De Quincey, still desperately in need of money, was forced to fall back upon the sort of literary projects he had advanced several years before in *The Westmoreland Gazette*. **11441**

The mature De Quincey, who in 1821 stood at the beginning of his long and active career as a literary journalist, brought to his work many extraordinary qualities. His intelligence was strong and keen, having been exercised for many years through extensive reading and daily intercourse with some of the finest minds in England. Never was there a writer—including even Coleridge himself—with a wider range of interests and sympathies or a greater capacity for illuminating the obscure reaches of scholarship with logic, imagination and passion. German philosophy and scholarship, the Greek and Latin classics, the literature of England from Chaucer down to the moderns, theology, political economy, literary criticism and theory, history, linguistics— all these subjects were within his purview. As for style, the continuous practice afforded by years and years of the sort of conversation that is really monologue, arranged and drawn out with the continuity and complexity of written discourse, had so cultivated his powers for disposing language that prose of the finest and most distinctive kind flowed from his pen with the fluency of speech.[30] The better part of *The Confessions of an English Opium Eater*, that incomparable display of stylistic virtuosity, was in fact written in the comparatively brief span of two months.[31] Nor was there wanting in De Quincey that strong commitment to matters of current interest which is the sustaining energy of the journalist. Although of retiring temperament and scholarly inclination, he always looked out upon the world with a lively interest in matters of current concern. Not only was he au courant of the new philosophy of Kant and poetry of Wordsworth and Coleridge, but he took a keen interest in contemporary politics. An avid reader of newspapers, he was always fascinated by the latest scandal, the latest crime, the latest bit of gossip—in short, all the motley stuff that goes to make up the news. Moreover, the task of writing for the public was not an uncongenial one for him. A certain didactic impulse in his nature made him ever eager to expound on any question within his competence to those readers—the merchants, the men of the professions, and especially the young people and the ladies—whose educations had not enabled them to read or understand the works of scholars and thinkers.[32]

Thomas De Quincey was an extraordinary man, a man of great parts, the sort of man from whom great things could be expected. Unfortunately, he was not a man of purpose. His vast accumulations of knowledge lay scattered and inert; his splendid style was merely an instrumentality; and his interest in things contemporary and his eagerness to please were not of themselves likely to lead him to some design worthy of his abilities. He had, of course, his little budget of literary projects—his translations, digests, and reports—which he first opened in the pages of *The Westmoreland Gazette*. To these he now added more of the same. In his notes of a conversation with De Quincey on November 3, 1821, a month after the publication of the second installment of the *Confessions*, Richard Woodhouse reports as follows:

I learned from him that he has several works in hand. He is about to write a few notes to Taylor's pamphlet [*The Restoration of National Prosperity shown to be immediately practicable*, London, 1821], for which purpose he is to have my interleaved copy. He is to write for the *London Magazine* an introduction to some English hexameters which he has composed; he is to write on the mode of reading Latin; on Kant's philosophy; on Coleridge's literary character; on Richter; to translate and abridge some tales from the German; to translate from the same an introduction to the weather observations and meteorological tables; to sketch out a closing address to the volume of the *London Magazine* ending December next, and give No. 3 of the Opium-Eater's "Confessions" for the February number; to write a series of letters to a young man of talent whose education had been neglected; to write on political economy.[33]

The obvious disparity between these humdrum literary labors and the splendidly imaginative character of the *Confessions of an English Opium Eater* requires no com-

ment. All of these projects, however, were perfectly legitimate undertakings, and they suggest De Quincey's earnest
endeavor in this period of his life to support himself by
bending his spirit to even the meanest tasks. To be sure,
even in this earliest period of his career, there was one
striking instance of plagiarism, which is usually passed over
as nothing more than an innocent lapse of memory. In the
little paper on Malthus, published in *The London Magazine* in 1823, De Quincey expounded an idea he had taken
from a book by Hazlitt, to which he made no acknowledgment.[34] In the next issue of the magazine there appeared
a courteously written letter from Hazlitt to the editor
claiming the credit for the idea.[35] De Quincey immediately
replied in a letter that is both evasive and unpleasant, but
contains, amid a host of sophistic excuses, a concession to
Hazlitt's claims.

It might be well at this point to mention that a number of De Quincey's leading ideas were derived from contemporary thinkers, especially from Wordsworth, whose
conversation De Quincey had enjoyed for many years, and
who, as modern scholars have come to recognize, was a
critical thinker frequently as profound and original as Coleridge, to whom, according to the old view of the matter,
Wordsworth stood indebted for ideas as a poet instructed
by a philosopher. The two great literary concepts usually
associated with the name of Thomas De Quincey—the distinction between the literature of power and the literature
of knowledge, and the theory of style as the incarnation
of thought—had in point of fact been derived, according
to De Quincey's own statement, from Wordsworth.[36] This
is not to say, of course, that the elaboration of these
ideas—their full development as hypotheses—was not in
large measure De Quincey's own accomplishment. But
here, as in many other instances, De Quincey simply served
as the agent for developing and expounding the views of
a more original mind.

Aside from the one obvious instance of plagiarism from Hazlitt, and a few other matters of minor importance, the writings of De Quincey's first period, the period of his connection with *The London Magazine*, are free of those illicit borrowings so common in his later work. However, as the years wore on, De Quincey, now a resident of Edinburgh and a writer for *Blackwood's Edinburgh Magazine*, began slowly to sink under a heavy burden of financial responsibility, ill-health, and spiritual distress. As he never earned enough by his writings to support his increasing family, his debts steadily mounted until he was "put to the horn"[37] and forced to seek sanctuary in Holyrood, when a fresh accumulation of debts soon drove him forth once again. For years he was a homeless and desperate man, harried constantly by bailiffs, living furtively in holes and corners—conditions in which literary composition was almost impossible, almost unthinkable. At one point his plight became so desperate that he had not even sufficient clothing to go out from his lodgings. The tale of his financial difficulties reached, over a course of years, heroic proportions, becoming an "Iliad of woes." The worst effect of his indigence was that it deprived him of the means for working. His splendid library had long since been sacrificed for ready money, and now he was hard put to obtain even the few volumes he required for his work.[38]

Sickness as well as poverty caused De Quincey enormous suffering and for periods of time incapacitated him for writing. And to the ills of the flesh were added the far more sinister ills of the spirit. He felt that his mind had been irreparably damaged by the use of opium, as may be seen from the following letter (in which he is speaking of his book *The Logic of Political Economy*). After asserting that the substance of the book was sound—as well he might, for it was wholly derived from Ricardo—he goes on to make excuses for its poor arrangement:

But as to the method of presenting the distinctions, as
to the composition of the book, and the whole evolu-
tion of a course of thinking, there it is that I too deeply
recognize the mind affected by my morbid condition.
Through that ruin, and by the help of that ruin, I
looked into and read the latter states of Coleridge. His
chaos I comprehended by the darkness of my own, and
both were the work of laudanum. It is as if ivory carv-
ings and elaborate fretwork and fair enamelling should
be found with worms and ashes amongst coffins and the
wrecks of some forgotten life or some abolished nature.
In parts and fractions eternal creations are carried on,
but the nexus is wanting, and life and the central principle which should bind together all the parts at the
centre, with all its radiations to the circumference, are
wanting. Infinite incoherence, ropes of sand, gloomy incapacity of vital pervasion by some one plastic principle,
that is the hideous incubus upon my mind always.[39]

Whether the cause of De Quincey's difficulties was really
opium or whether it was some more profound psychological
disturbance such as might in turn explain the initial craving for opium, the fact remains that in his high maturity
his nervous system was terribly deranged. He had developed
a peculiar neurosis which made writing an occasion of fear-
ful agony and eventually made it impossible for him to
contemplate even the writing of a little note without
anxiety and loathing. In a letter to Miss Mitford from
the year 1846 he gives a graphic description of his affliction:

No purpose could be answered by my vainly endeav-
ouring to make intelligible for my daughters what I
cannot make intelligible for myself—the undecipherable
horror that night and day broods over my nervous system. One effect of this is to cause, at certain intervals,
such whirlwinds of impatience as precipitate me vio-
lently, whether I will or not, into acts that would seem

insanities, but are not such in fact, as my understanding is never under any delusion. Whatever I may be writing becomes suddenly overspread with a dark frenzy of horror. I am using words, perhaps, that are tautologic; but it is because no language can give expression to the sudden storm of frightful revelations opening upon me from an eternity not coming, but past and irrevocable. Whatever I may have been writing is suddenly wrapt, as it were, in one sheet of consuming fire—the very paper is poisoned to my eyes. I cannot endure to look at it, and I sweep it away into vast piles of unfinished letters, or inchoate [sic] essays begun and interrupted under circumstances the same in kind, though differing unaccountably in degree. I live quite alone in my study, so nobody witnesses these paroxysms. Nor, if they did, would my outward appearance testify to the dreadful transports within.[40]

Given these various indications of the desperate conditions under which De Quincey lived, it becomes immediately apparent that De Quincey's tendency to plagiarize and his incapacity for original work were in part the products of his circumstances. In fact, one wonders how he was able to work at all, assailed as he was so fantastically from both within and without. One must assume that his writings were produced by fits and starts, concocted during the momentary lulls between those whirlwinds of impatience and irritability of which he complains. He struggled fitfully to maintain his pose of scholarly erudition, pressing into service such random materials as fell in his way, writing frequently from imperfect memories of reading done in better days many years before, working ingeniously around the vast gaps in his knowledge, and expatiating gratefully upon those points for which he was adequately prepared. It was all a desperate pretense and an audacious hoax. He had never been a well-built scholar; nor was he

an original thinker, or even a man of elaborate and sys-
tematic tastes. His imagination could respond only to
stimulations from without, and then the response was
likely to be brief and exaggerated. But at all times he was
supported by a strong sense of his own worth and an
unfailing stylistic ability that enhanced even the most
meager materials. The tone of authority he so confidently
struck in everything he wrote served to awe editors and
readers, who could not but believe that a man who expressed himself so naturally ex cathedra had somehow at
his command infinite resources of knowledge and erudition.
Few people indeed were prepared to challenge his favorite
journalistic pose as polyhistor, or universal authority on
matters of intellectual or scholarly interest.

The Polyhistor

ALL THE VIRTUES that distinguish Thomas De Quincey as
a scholar are brilliantly displayed in his long and illuminating account of the life and works of Richard Bentley,
the great English classicist.[1] This elaborate and polished
composition is offered as an original exposition of a difficult scholarly topic by a writer who is easily conversant
with the primary materials as well as the dependent scholarship, and speaks with great authority, though condescend-
ing for the occasion to employ arguments and language
intelligible to a layman.

Unlike so many of De Quincey's papers, this treatment
of Bentley, although extending to one hundred and twenty
pages, is closely woven in its design and texture, forthright
in its tone, and fully sustained from beginning to end by
a firm and comprehensive grasp of the factual materials. In
praising the "Bentley," Edward Sackville-West, De Quincey's most discerning critic, stresses its excellence as composition and its impressiveness as scholarship: "Admiration
in this case brought with it a greater degree of concentration on the object than De Quincey usually commanded;
the essay is extremely well knit, and free of digressions,
while the examination of Bentley's work gives a very good
idea of De Quincey's own minute and anxious scholarship."[2] David Masson likewise places a high value on this
"long and scholarly paper, the most elaborate of all De
Quincey's efforts of the strictly biographical kind, and a

really important contribution to English biographical literature."[3]

The paper is arranged in three independent sections:
Part i is a full and circumstantial account of Bentley's
life; Part ii, a critical resumé of his scholarly works; Part
iii, an "analysis" of Bentley's famous *Dissertation upon
the Epistles of Phalaris*. Originally published in the form
of two successive articles in *Blackwood's Edinburgh Magazine* for September and October, 1830, this essay had as
its occasion the publication of a new biography of Bentley
by James Henry Monk, D.D. De Quincey was probably
assigned to review the book, but he makes no effort to
characterize or evaluate it as a whole. Instead, after a very
casual reference to Dr. Monk's work,[4] he immediately
proceeds to his own account of Bentley's life and writings.
This practice was common in the reviews of that period. In
fact, the tendency to ignore the functions of a reviewer
in favor of those of an original author was so extreme
that it provoked sharp criticism from editors and readers
alike.[5]

In this instance, however, there can be little doubt
about what De Quincey thought of Dr. Monk's biography,
even though he never confronts the book directly. On almost every page he makes, *en passant*, some slighting remark on the author's scholarship, critical judgment, or
expository ability: Dr. Monk is careless of chronology; he
frequently contradicts himself; he has blundered in con-
struing a Greek passage; he entertains too high an opinion
of Colbatch, Bentley's most inveterate enemy; his estimate
of Bentley's character is that of a copy-book moralist.[6] The
effect of these constant criticisms, so vigorously articulated
and so triumphantly driven home, is naturally strongly
negative. The final effect is to make the reader feel that
Dr. Monk is a very indifferent scholar and expositor, that
he stands continually in need of correction by a mind
more refined and better informed, and that, in short, his

book has served De Quincey merely as a convenient foundation for rearing an independent presentation of Bentley's career and a more sophisticated appraisal of his achievements.

There are, however, certain unmistakable signs of dependency that disturb this otherwise uniform impression of authority and originality. In his narrative of Bentley's life, De Quincey is evidently drawing much of his material from Monk. Before commencing on the famous quarrel between Bentley and the Fellows of Trinity College, he writes: "I shall give a faithful abstract of its revolutions, condensed from many scores of pages in Dr. Monk's quarto." (iv, 148) This is certainly not the language of an independent authority, and doubts about De Quincey's originality begin to make themselves felt.

After reading De Quincey, who gives such a negative impression of Monk, one is clearly not prepared to find the Doctor's book anything like a successful treatment of its subject. But *The Life of Richard Bentley, D.D.* (London, 1830), it turns out, is a work of elaborate and intelligent research—clear, objective, and exhaustive. Dr. Monk had gone into his subject in great depth: many of the documents upon which his study is based—letters, college records, legal memoranda—he discovered and published for the first time. He was especially well versed in the history of the English colleges and their peculiar statutes and institutions; and for an author of a life of Bentley, this is a matter of the utmost importance since the great scholar, who for thirty years was Master of Trinity College, was throughout his career embroiled in legal disputes arising out of his reforms and modifications of the College's laws and practices. It must be clear, even on this brief statement of the case, that a disinterested writer reviewing this admirable book, which is still the only authoritative work on the subject, could not do less than praise it generously and commend it to his readers.

When the article is compared with the book, it becomes evident that De Quincey is slavishly dependent on Monk, not only for his information about Bentley's life but for his knowledge of Bentley's works as well (the dissertation on Phalaris alone excepted). As regards the life, De Quincey's every fact concerning Bentley's birth, rearing, education, appointments, honors, and professional activities has been derived from Monk. He has likewise appropriated from the Doctor all the laboriously assembled details of thirty years of legal processes, along with the facts of the Phalaris Controversy—that celebrated episode in the Quarrel of the Ancients and the Moderns. Similarly, to Monk can be traced all those impressive allusions which De Quincey so confidently makes to other classical scholars—to Lenep, Middleton, Vissius, Graevius, Kuster, Le Clerc, and Spanheim. And his dependency extends even to those small matters of incidental importance which, though not essential to the narrative, nonetheless give it its air of comprehensive knowledge. At one point, for example, De Quincey remarks that the sermon which Corporal Trim reads in *Tristram Shandy* is actually a genuine sermon composed by Bentley. (IV, 184) This is just the sort of information one naturally expects from De Quincey's universal curiosity; the fact, however, is also reported by Monk.[7]

However, it is not so much the extent of De Quincey's indebtedness in the biographical portion of his paper that is surprising, as it is the hoax he perpetrates in undertaking to review critically all of Bentley's numerous and multifarious works when apparently he had no more knowledge of them than could be gleaned from the incidental notices of these works woven into Monk's narrative. This resumé is the most impressive display of scholarly erudition to be found in any of De Quincey's writings. For over twenty pages he astounds the reader with his minute and exact knowledge of what seems an endless series of lectures, sermons, treatises, prolegomena, dissertations, editions, and proposals for learned works.[8] Once one begins to look for such things, it becomes apparent that De Quincey frequently declines the opportunity to criticize Bentley's work, and contents himself with a recital of the circumstances that occasioned the piece under discussion. Of this sort of material he found a great abundance in Monk; he had only to make a selection from it to appear a master of his subject.

The third part of De Quincey's paper is an "analysis"—that is to say, a précis—of Bentley's most famous work, the *Dissertation upon the Epistles of Phalaris*. How De Quincey obtained a copy of this work is uncertain, but a comparison of the précis with the dissertation strongly suggests that he had the book open before him as he wrote. Not only has De Quincey outlined the various arguments so clearly that they can be understood by even a casual reader; he has also managed to convey the interest and excitement of actually reading this remarkable *tour de force* of classical scholarship.

After examining De Quincey's most brilliant paper on a scholarly theme, what emerges is the fact that the entire composition is simply a sequence of skillfully drawn and impressively mounted abstracts. By adopting the tone of an authority and by sinking the real authority below our consideration, De Quincey easily persuades his readers that he is speaking from a firsthand acquaintance with his subject. The illusion is so perfect that it has beguiled even such close students of De Quincey's work as Masson and Sackville-West.[9]

Even if one considers it legitimate for De Quincey to offer an unacknowledged abstract as a book review, one cannot extend this allowance to his other scholarly works, which likewise are frequently unacknowledged abstracts.

The technique that produced the life of Bentley was also involved in De Quincey's life of Pope, which was written in 1837 and designed for inclusion in the seventh edition of the *Encyclopaedia Britannica*.[10] De Quincey was at one with Byron in defending Pope against his Romantic detractors. He claimed to have studied Pope very carefully, "with the purpose of becoming his editor." It is therefore natural that the thoroughgoing exposition of Pope's life and circumstances contained in the *Britannica* article should be treated by students of De Quincey's work as if it were a genuine product of scholarship. John E. Jordan has described this efficient biographical essay as follows: "As a short biography, De Quincey's effort is on the whole fresh, appreciative, and well-balanced; commendably free from digression, it sticks to ascertainable facts and is wanting chiefly in its failure to pay attention to the women in the poet's life. The paper has the special merit of considering Pope in relation to his time and environment, not ignoring the particular effects of his religion, his infirmity, and his education."[11]

Professor Jordan might also have said that this account was evidently written with a full knowledge of all the primary materials for a life of Pope. There are frequent citations from Pope's letters and from the letters of his friends—Martha Blount, Dr. Arbuthnot, Dean Swift; and proper use is made of the *Anecdotes* of Spence and the early lives of Ruffhead, Warton, and Warburton, as well as the later and more critical accounts of Johnson and Bowles.[12]

However, these appearances of scholarly industry are deceptive, since upon investigation it turns out that De Quincey's knowledge was most probably derived second hand, and from a single book the use of which he fails to acknowledge.

The clue to De Quincey's source in this case is provided by two very curious allusions to a certain "Mr. Roscoe." Near the beginning of his account, in speaking of Pope's education, he says, "Mr. Roscoe speaks of Pope's personal experience as necessarily unfavourable to public schools; but in reality he knew nothing of public schools." (IV, 241) Of this Roscoe nothing further is heard for more than twenty pages until abruptly, in the midst of a discussion of Pope's translation of the *Odyssey*, Roscoe again appears: "The 'Odyssey' was commenced in 1723 (not 1722, as Mr. Roscoe virtually asserts at p. 259)." (IV, 265)

At first these two allusions, so abruptly introduced and so inconsequential in their relation to the text, appeared to have no particular significance. However, tracing this allusion revealed that "Mr. Roscoe" was in fact William Roscoe, the great authority on Pope who in 1824 (thirteen years before De Quincey's paper) had issued a massive ten-volume edition of Pope's works, including in the initial volume the first full-scale life of the poet. The book ran to 585 pages including the appendices, which contain letters and documents of particular interest.[13]

De Quincey's allusions to Roscoe clearly imply that he had read the book; and, in fact, a comparison of De Quincey's account of Pope's life with Roscoe's immediately reveals that the latter was De Quincey's sole source, as the basic material was found in Roscoe. Indeed, there was no other place where De Quincey could have found some of the information, particularly that drawn from Pope's letters. Furthermore, the sympathetic and well-balanced tone of De Quincey's paper is in perfect accord with the character of Roscoe's book, which is similarly favorable to the poet and judicious in its treatment of the controversial passages in his life.

There are, of course, a few passages original with De Quincey, but these, as one would expect, are purely speculative. For example, Roscoe suggests that Pope received no formal education because "the disposition of Pope was not suited to compulsory modes of instruction."[14] De Quincey ignores this explanation and suggests otherwise:

> *Alexander Pope the elder was a man of philosophical de-*
> *sires and unambitious character. Quiet and seclusion and*
> *innocence of life,—these were what he affected for him-*
> *self; and that which had been found available for his own*
> *happiness he might reasonably wish for his son. The two*
> *hinges upon which his plans may be supposed to have*
> *turned were, first, the political degradation of his sect,*
> *and, secondly, the fact that his son was an only child. . . .*
> *Either his son, therefore, would be a rustic recluse, or,*
> *like himself, he would be a merchant. With such pros-*
> *pects, what need of an elaborate education?*
>
> (IV, 242–43)

Except for a few such speculative flights, De Quincey's
"Pope" is a straightforward exposition of the poet's life.
Again, as in the case of the "Bentley," De Quincey had before him while writing this article a full and scholarly treatment of the subject. And again, his method was simply the
abstraction of all the principal matters of interest so as to
provide his readers with a concise and accurate account. Because he had so much material from which to select, he was
able to treat the most interesting questions in fine detail.
Generally, it may be said that it was his practice in drawing
up these abstracts to omit much that was in the source, but
to reproduce almost verbatim the accounts of the most
interesting events.

Any reader of the life of Pope would naturally be curious
about the details of Pope's arrangements in making his
famous translations of Homer. And so in this particular,
De Quincey is very close to his source. Roscoe gives the
pertinent facts concerning the translation of the *Odyssey*
in these words:

> Of this translation, the first, fourth, nineteenth, and
> twentieth books, are the work of Fenton; the second,
> sixth, eighth, eleventh, twelfth, sixteenth, eighteenth, and
> twenty-third, are by Broome, and the remaining twelve
> by Pope. The notes were compiled by Broome, but the

postscript to them was written by Pope himself, and is considered by Dr. Warton as "a fine piece of criticism." According to Ruffhead, Pope gave Fenton six hundred pounds, and Broome three hundred for their trouble; but according to Warton, Fenton had only three hundred, and Broome five hundred, which from their respective shares in the work seems more likely to be the fact.[15]

De Quincey has merely rearranged and condensed this factual recital.

> But in this instance he had two coadjutors, Broome and Fenton: between them they translated twelve books, leaving twelve to Pope. The notes also were compiled by Broome; but the postscript to the notes was written by Pope. Fenton received £300, Broome £500. Such, at least, is Warton's account, and more probable than that of Ruffhead; who not only varies the proportions, but increases the whole sum given to the assistants by £100.
>
> (IV, 263)

That De Quincey in his scholarly papers should have resorted to the techniques of a hack writer now appears as the inevitable consequence of his want of the requisite learning for such taxing themes. Yet that he should, on occasion, have employed the same devices in the composition of his personal memoirs, the narrative of his own life, must strike one as a surprising and wholly unexpected fact, a fact requiring a rather different sort of explanation.

It is one of the most curious features of De Quincey's development as a writer that, after commencing his career so auspiciously with a masterpiece of autobiography, he should have spent so many years exploring every other department of literature, never once returning to his major theme.

When, in 1834, thirteen years after the appearance of the *Confessions*, De Quincey began to publish his "Autobiographic Sketches,"[16] he was no longer the unspoiled amateur who had poured out so heedlessly all his best material for a mere forty pounds. Now he was a seasoned, if not a hardened, journalist, fully conscious of the danger of expending himself too freely. And so one finds in these "Autobiographic Sketches" an entirely different method of presenting his life experiences. No longer does he aspire to "a mode of impassioned prose"; rather, what comes through now seems to be the dry voice of an aged raconteur—a very self-conscious man of letters, quite confident of his ability to hold the attention of his readers even when relating the most trivial incidents. And one is conscious now of a mind constantly alert to the opportunities any narrative provides for digression, descriptive elaboration and all the other devices that avail for filling up space and padding pages.[17]

In his "Autobiographic Sketches" De Quincey appears to have adopted a deliberate policy of economy. But, in addition to economy, there was another means that he sometimes employed to extend his rather limited resources. When the occasion offered, he could interpolate in the account of his life various matters, interesting enough in themselves, which, though forming no part of his actual experience, could upon various pretexts be made to fit within the general framework of autobiography. In these interpolated papers, of which there are four—the two essays on the Irish Rebellion of 1798[18] and the accounts of George and Sarah Green and of Elizabeth Smith—De Quincey has proceeded in exactly the same manner as in his so-called scholarly reviews: abstracting his material from books and presenting it as original work.

When in the course of the "Autobiographic Sketches" De Quincey comes to the journey to Ireland that he took in his sixteenth year, he introduces into the rather meager account of his actual experiences in Ireland a full-scale narrative of the events of the Irish Insurrection which had occurred in 1798, just two years before his visit. He offers as his reason for narrating this history the fact that, while in Ireland, he had collected from various people who had actually participated in the hostilities a number of interesting stories and descriptions.[19] In this, of course, there is nothing that would challenge the reader's skepticism. When one comes to read the papers, however, the treatment of the events they contain is so complete and so masterful in its presentation of detail, that one instantly suspects a hoax. And, furthermore, a letter that survives from this very period makes it clear that, although the young De Quincey had gone to Ireland expecting to learn many exciting details of the war, he had in fact been utterly disappointed by the disparaging way in which everyone alluded to the action— as if it had been a mere Birmingham riot.[20]

It is apparent, then, that for both of these papers he must have had an adequate source; both can be traced to what was probably the standard history of the Rebellion in De Quincey's day: the Reverend James Gordon's *History of the Rebellion in Ireland in the Year 1798*.[21]

De Quincey's first paper, which recounts vividly and concisely the events of the principal insurrection in the County of Wexford, is simply a skillful précis of the first chapters of Gordon's *History*. Commencing near the beginning of Gordon's book with the circumstances that led up to the insurrection, De Quincey follows his original, section by section—from the description of the secret Irish patriotic organizations and the exposure of the plot of the United Irishmen, through the whole course of the hostilities, beginning with the capture of Enniscorthy and ending with the final battle and defeat of the rebels at Vinegar Hill. Not only has he followed his source in every detail and in the original order of exposition, but he has consistently maintained Gordon's point of view, and at times he is very close to the language of the original, as the following excerpts will demonstrate. Here is Gordon's account of the exposure of the secret Society of United Irishmen:

a very severe wound was inflicted on the union [of United Irishmen] by the arrest of the thirteen members composing the provincial committee of Leinster, with other principals of the conspiracy, at the house of Oliver Bond of Bridge-street, in Dublin, on the 12th of March. The arrest was grounded on the information of Thomas Reynolds, a Roman Catholic gentleman, of a place called Kilkea-Castle, in the county of Kildare, colonel of an United Irish regiment, treasurer of the county of Kildare, and provincial delegate for Leinster, who having travelled in the same carriage with William Cope, a wealthy and respectable merchant of Merrion-square, in Dublin, about the twenty-fifth of the preceding month, had been induced by the arguments of that gentleman, and the picture which he drew of the horrors of a revolutionary war in Ireland, to disclose for the use of government what he knew of the conspiracy—pretending, however, to receive from time to time his information from another person, not to be himself the original informer.—In this arrest were included the most able and active leaders of the union—Thomas Addis Emmet, a lawyer of prime abilities; Doctor William James M'Nevin; Arthur O'Connor, and Oliver Bond. The vacancies made in the directory and elsewhere, by the seizure of these and other persons, were quickly filled, but with men less fit for the arduous attempt of overturning an old government, and establishing a new. To prevent a despondency among the members of the union on this occasion, a hand-bill, dated St. Patrick's day, the seventeenth of March, was distributed etc.[22]

Now here is De Quincey:

A treacherous or weak brother, high in the ranks of the society, and deep in their confidence, happened, when travelling up to Dublin in company with a Royalist, to speak half mysteriously, half ostentatiously, upon the delicate position which he held in the councils of his dangerous party. This weak man, Thomas Reynolds, a Roman Catholic gentleman, of Kilkea Castle, in Kildare, colonel of a regiment of United Irish, treasurer for Kildare, and

in other offices of trust for the secret society, was prevailed on by William Cope, a rich merchant of Dublin,
who alarmed his mind by pictures of the horrors attending
a revolution under the circumstances of Ireland, to betray
all he knew to the government. His treachery was first
meditated in the last week of February 1798; and, in consequence of his depositions, on March 12, at the house of
Oliver Bond, in Dublin, the government succeeded in
arresting a large body of the leading conspirators. The
whole committee of Leinster, amounting to thirteen
members, was captured on this occasion; but a still more
valuable prize was made in the persons of those who pre-
sided over the Irish Directory—viz., Emmet, M'Niven,
Arthur O'Connor, and Oliver Bond. As far as names
went, their places were immediately filled up; and a hand-
bill was issued, on the same day, with the purpose of in-
tercepting the effects of despondency amongst the great
body of the conspirators. But Emmet and O'Connor were
not men to be effectually replaced.

(1, 232–33)

It is clear that De Quincey's own contribution to this
passage is, to put it charitably, slight.

In his paper dealing with the French landing on the west
coast of Ireland later in the same year (1798), and the subsequent insurrection of the Irish peasantry in Connaught, De
Quincey has proceeded, as on other occasions, by pretending
a familiarity with the original materials, when in fact his
knowledge was derived from a secondary source. In this case
he presents a number of extracts from an obscure pamphlet
written by an Irish Bishop who had been captured by the
French, and who was an eye witness to their operations in
the town of Killala.[23] This pamphlet is extensively quoted
over a space of almost thirty pages at the end of Gordon's
History. All of De Quincey's extracts from it are found in
Gordon, and the running commentary with which De Quin-

cey has sustained and integrated these extracts turns out to be merely a paraphrase of other passages in the pamphlet reproduced by Gordon.

There is absolutely nothing in the forty-odd pages of De Quincey's two essays that is original with him—either in the way of additional information not to be found in Gordon or of comment or speculation upon the events of the history.

In the papers hitherto considered, De Quincey's sources were all substantial works, fully adequate for the purpose he had in mind. Fortified with a book like Monk's *Life of Richard Bentley*, a writer of De Quincey's ability could easily pass as an authority on his subject. Sometimes, however, he was not so fortunate as to possess the sort of book which he needed, and in these cases he was reduced to desperate expedients. In the next section a group of papers which were derived from sources utterly inadequate for the purpose envisaged will be considered.

2

In addition to the "Pope," De Quincey wrote three other lives for the seventh edition of the *Encyclopaedia Britannica—Goethe, Schiller,* and *Shakespeare.* The life of Goethe[24] has been criticized as inadequate,[25] and indeed it leaves much to be desired. As always, De Quincey was relying on a single book for his information, and, as numerous references to Goethe's "Memoirs" make clear, that book was *Dichtung und Wahrheit.* Goethe's autobiography is a very substantial work, but for a writer of the poet's life it has been one great disadvantage—it breaks off abruptly with Goethe's departure for the Ducal Court at Weimar, which occurred in his twenty-sixth year. Now as Goethe lived to be eighty-three, and as almost all of his important works with the exception of *Götz von Berlichingen* and *Werther* were written after the time of his arrival at Weimar, it is obvious that a writer relying exclusively on this work would be hard put to fill in most of the outline of the poet's life.

De Quincey can hardly be said to have overcome this difficulty successfully. He begins well enough, writing the wonderfully firm and full prose that one always encounters in his works of abridgment; and, as is characteristic of his short-sighted planning, he commences on a scale so large that it would have taken him a couple of hundred pages to sum up Goethe's six hundred. But as he proceeds, his pace accelerates until at the end the events are whirling by at such a rate that the impression is simply one of a blur. Many of the important events that occupy the later books of *Dichtung und Wahrheit* are omitted entirely, and so nothing is heard of Frederika Brion or Lili Schönemann, nothing of Goethe's years at the University of Strassburg, or of his relationship with Herder. Having crammed the final books of *Dichtung und Wahrheit* into a few pages, De Quincey terminates his account just where one might have expected—with the departure of Goethe for Weimar.

At this point his material was exhausted, though he still had the better part of the life to write, as well as the customary critical estimate of the poet's writings and reputation. Unable to continue, he impudently informs his readers:

> The life of Goethe was so quiet and so uniform after the year 1775, when he may first be said to have entered into active life by taking service with the Duke of Weimar, that a biographer will find hardly any event to notice, except two journeys to Italy, and one campaign in 1792, until he draws near the close of his long career. It cannot interest an English reader to see the dates of his successive appointments. It is enough to know that they soon raised him to as high a station as was consistent with literary leisure, and that he had from the beginning enjoyed the unlimited confidence of his sovereign.
>
> (IV, 415)

This conclusion, which reminds one of nothing so much as of a fairy tale, and which has about the same degree of truth, is De Quincey's substitute for all the important events of Goethe's mature life. As for the conventional critical estimate, that he dispenses with in much the same offhand manner. One page of vague prose suffices for the novels, another cloudy page disposes of the plays. *Faust* is put aside with the consoling remark that, "Upon this it is better to say nothing than too little. How trifling an advance has been made towards clearing the ground for any sane criticism may be understood from this fact, that as yet no two people have agreed about the meaning of any separate scene, or about the drift of the whole." (IV, 418)

De Quincey concludes with the gratuitous observation that had Goethe "been called to face great afflictions, singular temptations, or a billowy and agitated course of life, our belief is that his nature would have been found unequal to the strife." (IV, 419)

Although it is hard to believe possible, the life of Schiller[26] is an even more irresponsible performance. One cannot speak of sources for a life that was never written; yet the one or two little bits of information De Quincey does offer his readers concerning the life of Schiller have a very amusing relation to their "source."

First, however, it is worth noting how De Quincey fills up the seventeen pages that the life of Schiller occupies in the standard edition. The first ten pages contain a very generalized account of the development of German literature from the late seventeenth century down to the period of Schiller's youth. It would appear that this little history of German literature is a by-product of De Quincey's reading *Dichtung und Wahrheit*, which is, in addition to being an autobiography, perhaps the most astute history ever written of German culture for a period of over a hundred years. However, such a generalized resumé might have been derived in other ways.

After these time-consuming preliminaries, De Quincey finally commences his life, devoting a disproportionate amount of space to Schiller's parents, about whom he seems to have learned a thing or two from the little life by Heinrich Doering, which served also as the foundation for Carlyle's *Life of Schiller*.[27] De Quincey quotes, for example, a very eloquent prayer that Schiller's father is supposed to have offered up at the birth of his son:

Oh, God, that knowest my poverty in good gifts for my son's inheritance, graciously permit that, even as the want of bread became to thy Son's hunger-stricken flock in the wilderness the pledge of overflowing abundance, so likewise my darkness may, in its sad extremity, carry with it the measure of thy unfathomable light; and, because I, thy worm, cannot give to my son the least of blessings, do thou give the greatest; because in my hands there is not anything, do thou from thine pour out all things; and that temple of a new-born spirit, which I cannot adorn even with earthly ornaments of dust and ashes, do thou irradiate with the celestial adornment of thy presence, and finally with that peace that passeth all understanding.

(IV, 432)

As Schiller's father was a humble forester and not a man of education or literary talents, such a prayer must strike one as being extremely anachronistic. It is, in fact, an invention of De Quincey's (a very characteristic bit of rewriting, by the way). The original passage in Doering runs as follows:

In an essay still extant, he [the father] expresses himself on this matter in a heart-felt and touchingly pious manner: "And you Being of all Beings! I asked you after the birth of my only son that you would add those powers of intellect I could not attain for want of instruction. You hearkened to me. Thank you, kindest of beings, for heeding the prayers of mortals."[28]

All that directly pertains to the life of Schiller is contained in the last five pages of the article. This includes a substantial quotation from Schiller (also extracted from Doering) concerning his confined circumstances and disturbed state of mind during the composition of *The Robbers*. De Quincey concludes by mentioning the titles of some of Schiller's best-known plays, and by characterizing briefly the effect made by *The Robbers* on its first appearance.

It is perhaps worth remarking that in both the "Goethe" and the "Schiller" De Quincey writes as though he were really ignorant of these writers' works and was obliged to bluff; whereas, in fact, he had reviewed *Wilhelm Meister* in the Carlyle translation some years before and he had read with admiration Coleridge's translation of *Wallenstein*.[29] It may be assumed that he was familiar with *Werther* and with the *Fiesco*.[30] It would appear that on occasions like these De Quincey's good sense completely left him and he suffered from a strange absence of mind.

The life of Shakspeare[31] is essentially different from the other lives he wrote for the *Encyclopaedia Britannica*. Whereas the intention in the "Pope," the "Goethe," and the "Schiller" was simply to present the circumstances of the author's life with a few critical remarks upon his work, the "Shakspeare" [*sic*] was conceived with a more ambitious purpose. De Quincey's intention as well as his factual sources are revealed in the letter which he wrote to Adam Black, the publisher of the *Encyclopaedia*, on July 16, 1838. After complaining that "no paper ever cost me so much labour," he goes on:

> *I anticipate your approval of this article . . . no one question has been neglected which I ever heard of in connexion with Shakespeare's name; and I fear no rigour of examination, notwithstanding I have had no books to assist me but the two volumes lent me by yourself (viz. 1st vol. of Alex. Chalmer's edit. 1826, and the late popular edit. in one vol. by Mr. Campbell).*[32]

De Quincey's life of Shakespeare is largely speculative, partly because he was concerned to express himself on a variety of controversial questions and partly, it does not seem too much to suggest, because the source material which was available to him was utterly inadequate for the sort of abstract he produced in his other lives. Thomas Campbell's preface, "Remarks on the Life and Writings of William Shakespeare,"[33] contains a very sketchy treatment of Shakespeare's life. It does, however, provide two important documents: Shakespeare's marriage license bond and his will. De Quincey was particularly excited by the former document, which had only recently been discovered and which clearly implied that Shakespeare, like De Quincey himself, had been compelled to marry a woman to protect her reputation. Clearly, De Quincey's speculations on this subject are disguised expressions of his own feelings.

It would be tedious to enumerate all the various details De Quincey took directly from Campbell and Chalmers. More important though, is the recognition that De Quincey's paper may have assumed its loose and digressive form because it was not produced by the same processes that characterize the lives previously discussed. Without a substantial quantity of information to abridge, De Quincey was compelled to tack and veer, to seize upon every opportunity for divagation, to protract his discussion of each question far beyond the appropriate limit. Thus, he consumes fifteen pages in a very tenuous argument to establish that Shakespeare was not neglected in his own day. Two full pages are devoted to the question of whether or not Shakespeare was a gentleman; and, as has already been suggested, the discussion of Shakespeare's marriage goes far beyond the bounds established by the few pertinent facts. On the other hand, it is very significant that De Quincey, a life-long student of Shakespeare and one of his Romantic idolators, should neglect, or at least employ so inadequately, the opportunity this paper afforded him to discuss Shakespeare's works. He does throw out a few interesting suggestions on the contrast between Shakespearean tragedy and Greek tragedy, and on the valedictory implications of *The Tempest*. But even here he seems to be echoing other critics. Especially in his treatment of *The Tempest*, he is merely expanding a suggestion in Campbell, who advanced the familiar idea that *The Tempest* was Shakespeare's farewell to his art.

For a student of De Quincey's mind this failure to say something significant on a vast and familiar subject is extremely suggestive. It is another evidence of his strange incapacity to think at the right moment. In other essays dealing with other subjects, De Quincey has made many illuminating remarks on Shakespeare, and there is, of course, the inspired essay "On the Knocking at the Gate in Macbeth." But here, when directly confronted with the subject of Shakespeare's life and works, he suddenly has nothing to say, and he is forced to elaborate casuistically upon the meager facts adventitiously provided by his sources.[34]

It is now abundantly clear that in producing his scholarly papers De Quincey was frequently dependent upon source books, both for his leading ideas and for the factual materials necessary to substantiate his arguments or to elaborate his themes. As he did not scruple on occasion to abridge an entire book and put the abridgment forward as a product of original investigation, it is something of a mystery that in other similar articles he did not utilize to any great extent the factual materials of his sources. If he was willing to take some of the material, why did he not take all of it? Why was he sometimes reduced to desperate expedients to fill up articles which might have been crammed by simply taking more of the same sort of material?

Two articles, "The Pagan Oracles" and "Cicero,"[35] both written in 1842 and published in *Blackwood's Magazine*, will illustrate this peculiar relationship between some of De Quincey's compositions and their sources. In both of these pieces a classical subject is treated from what is purportedly an advanced or "paradoxical" point of view. The pagan oracles, for so many centuries the objects of Christian scorn and later of modern incredulity, are defended by De Quincey as useful political and social institutions. Cicero, the traditional model of Roman rectitude, is attacked as immoral and unpatriotic.

Casual allusions in each of these papers to recent works of foreign scholarship make it possible to trace the source for De Quincey's work. In the case of the paper on the pagan oracles, he had consulted P. van Limburg Brouwer's *Histoire de la Civilisation Morale et Religieuse des Grecs* (Groningue, 1840), particularly the twentieth and twenty-first chapters of the fourth volume, which contain a thorough treatment of the ancient oracles.[36] For the paper on Cicero he drew upon Bernard Rudolf Abeken's *Cicero in seinen Briefen* (Hanover, 1835), an exhaustive analysis of and commentary on the letters of Cicero, and a dense factual narrative of his life.[37]

Both of these books could easily have supplied matter for a dozen such articles; and yet in both papers De Quincey is clearly embarrassed for want of material, and is forced to overwork the small amount of information he does possess and to wrap it round with many layers of that fine-spun casuistical prose he invariably wrote when he had an inadequate command of his subject and was merely seeking to mask his ignorance by distracting the reader from the real requirements of the theme.

Thus, in "The Pagan Oracles" he begins by describing and evaluating a seventeenth century study on the subject by a certain Van Dale and then, entering upon the subject in his own right, he suddenly draws off from the announced theme and indulges himself in a series of digressive and irrelevant discussions of the nature of Christianity, the gradualness of historical change, and the true meaning of the term "prophecy" as it is employed in Hebrew literature. After many pages of this sort of disquisition, he finally turns to his subject and poses the following questions as a division of the topic: "1] What was the relation of the Oracles . . . to the religious credulity of Greece?   2] What was the relation of that same Oracle to absolute truth?   3] What was its relation to the public welfare of Greece?" (VII, 76) The discussion that follows these questions does contain some appropriate material in the form of Greek and Latin citations, illustrative cases, and suggestive anecdotes, all of it drawn from van Brouwer; but this material is very skimpy and its application by De Quincey is strained.

Now the corresponding discussion in van Brouwer's twenty-first chapter reaches a length of almost 150 pages, and its thoroughness may be gauged by the following syllabus printed at the head of the chapter:

> Examination of the responses given by the oracles . . .— On oracles that seem to contain a piece of advice or the confirmation of a question—Oracles containing internal evidence of their falseness—Oracles whose accomplishment may be attributed to chance—Oracles which by the manner of their wording were proven false by the event— Oracles whose accomplishment was owing to the priests' knowledge of the character and circumstances of the person consulting the oracle.[38]

As for the "paradoxical" point of view adopted by De Quincey in this paper, it is nothing more than an echo of van Brouwer's thesis, which is the defense of the oracles as institutions that contributed largely to the stability of Greek society, to the development of Greek civilization, and to the maintenance of moral and civic order. This thesis is: "I do not hesitate to add that, in general, it appears to me the oracles ranged themselves on the side of humanity, of good customs—in a word—public as well as private virtue; consequently, they exerted a salutary influence on the moral civilization of the Greeks."[39] Far from this being a novel or a paradoxical notion of pagan oracles in De Quincey's day, a comparable passage in Herder's *Ideen* would seem to indicate that this was the view entertained by most serious students of the subject at that time.[40]

In the case of the "Cicero" there appears the same tendency to draw away on the slightest pretext from the announced subject; a review of Cicero's life established grounds for De Quincey's assertion that Cicero was "deficient in the moral force and grandeur indispensable to one who aspired to control the age, or even to keep a proper place in it." (VI, 308) As in the paper on the oracles, De Quincey advances towards his theme through a long series of preliminary considerations, most of them quite wide of the mark. Thus, the reader is treated to a long attack upon the simplicity of traditional scholarship in its evaluation of the great figures of Roman history. This windy harangue culminates in a furious blast at Conyers Middleton (the author of a popular eighteenth-century life of Cicero), who is castigated as a free-thinker intent upon disparaging Christian ethics by holding up a falsely idealized personification of Roman morality. When at last De Quincey commits himself to his real subject, he offers a review of Cicero's actions during the time of the war between Caesar and Pompey. This review consumes twenty-five pages, and all the relevant material is drawn from Abeken. But on the whole it is strikingly deficient in factual matter. The few crumbs of information De Quincey possesses are padded out with long-winded digressions and far-fetched analogies.

De Quincey's hostile attitude toward Cicero was not derived from Abeken's book, which, as a sound and scholarly treatment of its subject, presents Cicero as constantly wavering and uncertain in his allegiances during this great crisis in Roman politics. De Quincey establishes his own version of the matter simply by ignoring completely one aspect of Abeken's evidence. And here again, as in his similarly prejudiced account of Bentley, one is made aware of the strangely warped character of De Quincey's intelligence.

The interesting problem for the student investigating

De Quincey's use of sources, however, is the mysterious lack of material in these papers, when, as has been shown, De Quincey was familiar with abundantly rich sources and when the lack of material seriously embarrassed him in the presentation of his subject.

This problem proved quite puzzling until the connection between it and a little note De Quincey appended to his series of articles on the Caesars (a series vitiated by the same insufficiency of material that characterizes the papers on the Oracles and on Cicero) became clear. Writing many years after the event, he says; "*The Caesars*, it may be right to mention, was written in a situation which denied me the use of books; so that, with the exception of a few penciled extracts in a pocket-book from the Augustan History, I was obliged to depend upon my memory for materials, in so far as respected facts." (vi, 418) As is known, at all times— even when his circumstances were most desperate—De Quincey carried about with him large quantities of manuscript, the threatened loss of which would wring cries of anguish from him.[41] It is known that one of his ways of working was to build up an article out of these pieces of manuscript, little slips of paper containing neatly written notes. Such a set of notes was published some years ago in *More Books* under the title "De Quincey on French Drama."[42] It is a fairly safe assumption that De Quincey was a poor note-taker, since he was always careless and disorganized in everything he did, and also since he placed great reliance upon his powers of memory. Therefore, it must frequently have happened that he let some book out of his hands, later needed for the making of an article, and was consequently forced to rely upon his scrappy notes and his general sense of the book's argument.[43] This would explain the sort of borrowing that has already been noticed in a piece like that on the pagan oracles in which, on the one hand, he adopts the general thesis of his source, and on the other hand, employs some small bits of factual matter, such as quotations and anecdotes and other little details that one would seek to preserve in a note. There thus emerges a rather curious picture of De Quincey as a man eager to borrow but balked by his own ineptness and carelessness, and almost compelled to be "original."

The most striking example of this dilemma is provided by the series of six articles entitled "The Caesars," a series that extends to the length of a small book.[44] "The Caesars" has sometimes been treated as an ambitious and serious work of historical analysis; and indeed, there are many passages in it that prompt this sort of criticism. Sackville-West, for example, finds much to praise in it and compares it with Montesquieu's *Considérations sur les Causes de la Grandeur et de la Décadence des Romains*.[45] Other critics, Oliver Elton among them, have dismissed it as unsound or treated it as a work of merely literary interest.[46]

Yet research would seem to demonstrate that it was not De Quincey's original intention in this work to write a monograph on the decline and fall of the Roman Empire; but rather that his intentions were far more appropriate to his limited resources—an anecdotal history of the private lives of the Caesars, based exclusively on Suetonius and Suetonius' successors, the Augustan historians. De Quincey has said as much in his introductory remarks to "The Caesars:"

> it is remarkable that no field has been less trodden than the private memorials of those very Caesars; whilst, at the same time, it is equally remarkable that precisely with the first of the Caesars commences the first page of what, in modern times, we understand by Anecdotes. Suetonius is the earliest writer in that department of Biography; so far as we know, he may be held first to have devised it as a mode of History, for he came a little before Plutarch. The six writers whose sketches are collected under the general title of the Augustan History followed in the same

*track. Though full of entertainment and of the most
curious researches, they are all of them entirely unknown,
except to a few elaborate scholars. We purpose to collect
from these obscure but most interesting memorialists a
few sketches and biographical portraits of those great
princes, whose public life is sometimes known, but very
rarely any part of their private and personal memoirs.*

(VI, 240–41)

"The Caesars," then, was intended as an abstract of certain ancient historians whose work was unknown to the general public. It was to be a study in "secret records." And it was to be a work of "anecdotage." The retelling of gossipy anecdotes was one of De Quincey's surest and most characteristic literary resources; it is, in fact, the method of all his famous papers on his contemporaries—Wordsworth, Coleridge, Lamb, Christopher North, etc.[47] If all had gone well, the work might have turned out to be a little masterpiece. It could have had the vividness and the humor of the "Last Days of Kant," the closely woven narrative force of the "Life of Bentley," and it might even have risen at moments to the heights De Quincey was later to achieve in his "Tartar Tribe." Certainly the material was enormously abundant and perfectly suited to his purposes. Moreover, it was familiar material: the Augustan historians are known to have been among De Quincey's favorite reading.[48] Several brilliant works have been mined from Suetonius, and these Augustan historians are in some respects an even richer repository of racy incidents and lurid descriptions. As the Augustan historians are still relatively obscure, perhaps it would not be unprofitable to pause briefly to sketch their character.[49]

The *Scriptores Augustanae Historiae* are titled in the principal manuscript (the Codex Palatinus) *Vitae Diversorum Principum et Tyrannorum a Divo Hadriano asque ad Numerianum Diversis Compositae;* but when Casaubon compiled his famous edition in the seventeenth century, he employed the title *Historia Augusta;* and ever since, the work of these writers has been known as the *Augustan History.* The collection of *Vitae,* which dates from the late third or early fourth century, is very extensive, occupying three volumes in the Loeb Classics edition and consisting of some thirty biographies, some of them double or triple lives, because it was the plan of the authors to include not only those Emperors who ruled, the *Augusti,* but also their heirs presumptive, the *Caesares,* and the principal claimants to the throne, the *Tyranni.* The professed model for these lives is Suetonius; but the work of the Augustan historians is much more gossipy, much less accurate (many forgeries of documents have been demonstrated), and the style, although just as concise, is far less polished. The outline of the various lives consists for the most part of the following categories: the ancestry of the Emperor, his life prior to his accession to the throne, his policy and the events of his reign, his personal traits, his death, his personal appearance, and his posthumous honors. As for the actual character of the material provided by these works, one cannot do better than De Quincey's own description in the "Philosophy of Roman History."

> It is impossible to conceive the dignity of History more degraded than by the petty nature of the anecdotes which compose the bulk of the communications about every Caesar, good or bad, great or little. They are not merely domestic and purely personal, when they ought to have been Caesarian, Augustan, Imperatorial: they pursue Caesar not only to his fireside, but into his bed-chamber, into his bath, into his cabinet, nay, even (sit honor auribus!) into his cabinet d'aisance; not merely into the Palatine closet, but into the Palatine water-closet. . . . with respect to the meals of Caesar;— what dishes, what condiments, what fruits, what confection prevailed at

each course; what wines he preferred; how many glasses
(cyathos) he usually drank; whether he drank more when
he was angry; Whether he diluted his wine with water;
half-and-half, or how?

(VI, 438)

One can easily imagine what De Quincey planned to
make of this material. He would have lavished all his art
upon it; and, to be sure, his work does contain a few superb
vignettes. There is, for instance, a beautifully evocative description of Caesar's crossing of the Rubicon; a jolly burlesque of Nero's far-fetched but futile efforts to assassinate
his mother; a horrific narrative of the same Emperor's last
days; the picturesque presentation of Commodus standing
in the amphitheatre and bringing down whole ranks of wild
beasts with his bow; and a grotesque description of the mad
revels of Caligula. But as a whole "The Caesars" must be
adjudged the most disappointing of De Quincey's longer
works. It has many serious defects, the most conspicuous
being the incongruity between its character as an anecdotal
history and its pretensions as a full-scale treatment of the
grand theme of decline and fall. De Quincey, one feels, is
constantly divagating from his true purpose and expending
himself upon a theme quite beyond his capacities. The work
is very badly planned. The first two lives, those of Julius
Caesar and Augustus, occupy a space disproportionate to
the length of the whole; and they themselves suffer from
an insufficiency of factual material. Far too much emphasis
is laid upon trivial questions of a statistical, legal, or socio-
logical order; and at the same time, much that demands
attention is glossed over or simply omitted. Of Suetonius'
twelve Caesars, for example, De Quincey treats only six. In
general, one feels the want of any supervening purpose or
control—every new paper seems to start off in a new direction.

The explanation of all these faults, one is led to believe,

is simply the fact that De Quincey could not carry out his original purpose with the materials he had at hand. And so he was compelled to dilute his anecdotal history with a large infusion of thin speculative writing—analyses and excursuses—which fail to interest as much as they fail to inform. He was compelled to write too much about the few figures with whom he was really familiar; he was forced to omit all those about whom he had no information. And as so many of his notes were drawn from the commentaries of Casaubon and Salmasius, which were appended to the text he had originally consulted,[50] his own essays are cluttered with boldly written disquisitions on statistics, Roman customs and law; in fine, all those questions that aroused the interest of the seventeenth-century commentators. He succeeded only when he remained true to his original intention of presenting anecdotes of the private lives of the Caesars; and in all of these, it can be shown, he is closely following the accounts contained in his sources.

Perhaps one substantial example will suffice to elucidate De Quincey's procedure in the most successful portions of his papers. Suetonius describes Nero's attempts to murder his mother thus:

> At last terrified by her violence and threats, he determined to have her life, and after thrice attempting it by poison and finding that she had made herself immune by antidotes, he tampered with the ceiling of her bedroom, contriving a mechanical device for loosening its panels and dropping them upon her while she slept. When this leaked out through some of those connected with the plot, he devised a collapsible boat, to destroy her by shipwreck or by the falling in of its cabin. Then he pretended a reconciliation and invited her in a most cordial letter to come to Baiae and celebrate the feast of Minerva with him. On her arrival, instructing his captains to wreck the galley in which she had come, by running into it as if by accident, he detained her at a banquet, and when she would return to Bauli, offered her his contrivance in place of the craft which had been damaged, escorting her to it

in high spirits and even kissing her breasts as they parted. The rest of the night he passed sleepless in intense anxiety, awaiting the outcome of his design. On learning that everything had gone wrong and that she had escaped by swimming, driven to desperation he secretly had a dagger thrown down beside her freedman Lucius Agermus, when he joyfully brought word that she was safe and sound, and then ordered that the freedman be seized and bound, on the charge of being hired to kill the emperor; that his mother be put to death, and the pretence made that she had escaped the consequences of her detected guilt by suicide.[51]

De Quincey is characteristically expansive and humorous:

On Agrippina, however, no changes in the poison, whether of kind or strength, had any effect; so that, after various trials, this mode of murder was abandoned, and the emperor addressed himself to other plans. The first of these was some curious mechanical device by which a false ceiling was to have been suspended by means of bolts above her bed, and in the middle of the night, the bolt being suddenly drawn, a vast weight would have descended with a ruinous destruction to all below. This scheme, however, taking air from the indiscretion of some amongst the accomplices, reached the ears of Agrippina; upon which the old lady looked about her too sharply to leave much hope in that scheme: so that also was abandoned. Next, he conceived the idea of an artificial ship, which, at the touch of a few springs, might fall to pieces in deep water. Such a ship was prepared, and stationed at a suitable point. But the main difficulty remained; which was to persuade the old lady to go on board. Not that she knew in this case who had been the ship-builder, for that would have ruined all; but it seems that she took it ill to be hunted in this murderous spirit, and was out of humour with her son; besides that any proposal coming from him, though previously indifferent to her, would have instantly become suspected. To meet this difficulty, a sort of reconciliation was proposed, and a very affectionate message sent, which had the effect of throwing Agrippina off her guard, and seduced her to Baiae for the purpose of joining the Emperor's party at a grand banquet held in commemoration of a solemn festival. She came by water in a sort of light frigate, and was to return in the same way. Meantime Nero tampered with the commander of her vessel and prevailed upon him to wreck it. What was to be done? The great lady was anxious to return to Rome, and no proper conveyance was at hand. Suddenly it was suggested, as if by chance, that a ship of the Emperor's, new and properly equipped, was moored at a neighboring station. This was readily accepted by Agrippina: the Emperor accompanied her to the place of embarkation, took a most tender leave of her, and saw her set sail. It was necessary that the vessel should get into deep water before the experiment could be made; and with the utmost agitation this pious son awaited news of the result. Suddenly a messenger rushed breathless into his presence, and horrified him by the joyful information that his august mother had met with an alarming accident, but, by the blessing of Heaven, had escaped safe and sound, and was now on her way to mingle congratulations with her affectionate son. The ship, it seems, had done its office; the mechanism had played admirably; but who can provide for everything. The old lady, it turned out, could swim like a duck; and the whole result had been to refresh her with a little sea-bathing. Here was worshipful intelligence. Could any man's temper be expected to stand such continued sieges? Money, and trouble, and infinite contrivance, wasted upon one old woman, who absolutely would not, upon any terms, be murdered! Provoking it certainly was; and of a man like Nero it could not be expected that he should any longer dissemble his disgust, or put up with such repeated affronts. He rushed upon his simple con-

gratulating friend, swore that he had come to murder him;
and as nobody could have suborned him but Agrippina,
he ordered her off to instant execution.

(vi, 287–89)

Comparison of De Quincey's narrative with its source
reveals his close dependence on the source at every point; it
also shows his concern for smooth and regular transitions
and his endeavor to clarify and heighten the action by slight
additions of appropriate details. It also becomes clear that
as he proceeds in his work, the incidents begin to assume in
his mind a farcical vividness, so that by the end of the anecdote he is playing the scene for laughs.

All of these practices will be more thoroughly examined
in the following chapter. But before leaving the subject of
De Quincey's classical scholarship, it is worth considering
briefly three other papers on classical themes which further
illustrate his dependence upon printed sources.

In the introduction to the "Philosophy of Herodotus,"[52]
De Quincey announces that he intends to vindicate Herodotus both as regards his reputation for veracity (which during the eighteenth century had descended so low that his
traditional title, Father of History, was mocked by one
wit, who called him Father of Lies) and in respect to his
principles of geography or "philosophy." The notion that
Herodotus, who traditionally had been admired as a stylist
but whose credulity had made him a laughing stock, could
be said to have had a "philosophy" was then a considerable
novelty; and one understands how modern critics in estimating this paper have considered it an important achievement. Sackville-West evidently investigated the history of
opinion on Herodotus quite thoroughly and found De
Quincey ahead of his time.

> The subject of Herodotus, again, is now in a very
> different position from that in which De Quincey found
> it. The recent excavations in the East and in Greece, the
> deciphering of hieroglyphs and cuneiform inscriptions,

have put us in a strong position from which to criticize Herodotus, and, since Sayce published his edition in the 'eighties, there has been an almost complete reversal of opinion in favor of Herodotus' veracity. It is now clear he preserved correctly some most valuable facts; that, even when he misunderstood them, the facts are still valuable and may be corrected from other sources; and that he was plainly influenced by Greek scientific ideas of the time. That being so, De Quincey's arguments are both sensible and acute; he understood very exactly the nature of Herodotus' work, and his . . . appreciation of his science has since received many justifications and is still doing so.[53]

Professor Eaton entertains a similar view: "one must admit that in such papers as that on the Essenes and that upon Herodotus, he is sympathetic with the growing scientific methods of the history of his time, with its close examination of sources and its willingness to revaluate and retest in a sceptical spirit earlier conclusions."[54]

The "Philosophy of Herodotus" begins with a series of random observations: There is an explanation of the true meaning of the title of Herodotus' work—'Ιστορια—which De Quincey explains means *investigations* not history; he also remarks on the confusion about Herodotus' measure of distance, the *stadium*; and he makes the rather whimsical suggestion that Herodotus be considered, not the Father of History, but the father of prose composition.

After these discursive remarks, De Quincey finally puts forward his most valuable materials which, as usual, he has carefully husbanded for the climax of his paper. These he casts into the form of four excursuses. The first is entitled: "The Non-Planetary Earth of Herodotus in its relation to the Planetary Sun." Under this heading De Quincey explains that Herodotus had no notion of the importance of latitude in determining temperature, but instead ascribed the seasonal variations in temperature to the effects of the winds. Moreover, De Quincey explains, this ignorance of latitude confuses the directional bearings in Herodotus, because the east is always determined by him from the position of the rising sun, which is fairly accurate in his native latitude of Greece, but quite inaccurate for positions substantially to the south or north. (VI, 113–18)

The second excursus is headed: "The Danube of Herodotus considered as a counterpole to the Nile." In this section De Quincey resolves one of the most perplexing problems in the study of the geography of Herodotus—his description of the course of the river Ister (Danube). By bringing to light certain assumptions fundamental to ancient geography, he proves that the confusion in Herodotus' account is caused by his conviction that the course of the Danube in the north must be a perfect counterpart to that of the Nile in the south. (VI, 118–23)

The third section is merely a correction of a verbal error found in discussions of Herodotus where the word "Africa" is employed by English translators for the Greek term "Lybia." The fourth section explains the concept of an *akté*, which is Herodotus' term for a large land mass, like Asia Minor, bounded on three sides by water and on the fourth by land—a term for which there is no exact equivalent in English. Herodotus imagined the relations of major geographical areas in terms of a balance of such *aktés*. (VI, 135–36)

Now, it is apparent that these geographical and climatological conceptions are such as would not be discovered by any ordinary student of the writings of Herodotus. The question is, to what extent are they original with De Quincey? Before presenting his technical excursuses, De Quincey states that

> what we propose to do is to bring forward two or three important suggestions of others not yet popularly known —shaping and pointing, if possible, their application—

brightening their justice, or strengthening their outlines.
And with these we propose to intermingle one or two
suggestions more exclusively our own.

(VI, 113)

These modest professions are De Quincey's substitute
for a proper acknowledgment of his real source for all the
leading ideas in his paper, a little book published about
this time by Hermann Bobrik entitled *Geographie des
Herodot*.[55] De Quincey alludes twice to Bobrik in his paper,
but not in such a way as to make clear his indebtedness to
him.[56] He apparently thought that Bobrik was a highly
original investigator, and therefore assumed that his presentation of the important ideas in Bobrik's book would
be a considerable novelty in England. In this, though, he
was completely mistaken. Bobrik was actually a rather
pedestrian and mechanical scholar, and his book is, for
the most part, simply a systemization of Herodotus' geographical notices. However, in his opening pages and once
toward the close, he introduces short discussions of general
principles which are all derived from one of the greatest
German scholars of this period, Barthold Georg Niebuhr.

In the annals of the *Königlich-Preussischen Akademie
der Wissenschaften* for the years 1812/13, there is a highly
original and brilliantly written dissertation which sets
forth in considerable detail all the ideas that De Quincey
received from Bobrik.[57] This dissertation, with another on
the same subject, had been translated into English and
published by the press of Oxford University in 1830—
that is, twelve years before the appearance of De Quincey's
paper.[58] Clearly, De Quincey is the most casual of classical
scholars.

One other source De Quincey drew on, especially for the
material in the first half of his paper, was Major James
Rennell's *The Geographical System of Herodotus* (London,
1830). De Quincey deals somewhat more openly with

Major Rennell, perhaps because he is not so seriously dependent upon him, or perhaps because the Major, knowing
no Greek, could be easily patronized.[59] However this may
be, all the ideas that are not derived from Bobrik De Quincey has taken from Rennell, so that in the final account
his own contribution to this subject amounts to very little
indeed.

At first sight there would not appear to be any need to
demonstrate a source for De Quincey's series of papers on
the Homeric question "Homer and the Homeridae."[60] The
reason for this is that in his introductory remarks in the first
of these three articles, De Quincey states quite frankly that
he intends to seat himself in the chair of the foremost
German authority on this subject, a certain Nitzsch, and expound the views of that scholar, which are inaccessible to
most readers, locked up as they are in the remote fastness
of an enormous German encyclopedia bearing the for-
bidding title *Allgemeine Encyklopädie der Wissenschaften
und Künste*. This unaccustomed show of ingenuousness,
however, proves to be a blind, for when one consults the
dusty volumes of the *Universal Encyclopedia*, one finds that
the article entitled "Homeros" was not written by Nitzsch,
who is in fact the author of a well-known commentary on
the *Odyssey*, but by an obscure person named Grotefend;
and there is no reason to believe De Quincey consulted this
article. De Quincey, in his series, carefully avoids the subject of the *Odyssey* and concentrates solely upon the *Iliad*.
It seems probable that De Quincey had never so much as
seen the encyclopedia he cites as his source.

The real truth of the matter is suggested by a letter
Professor Eaton quotes in the course of his biography. In
this letter, apparently addressed to William Blackwood,
De Quincey complains that the series on Homer had cost
him "more reading and of books the most confused than
any others he ever wrote." And in another letter to which
Professor Eaton alludes, De Quincey speaks of "five or six

books in this connection."[61] The author of the present study did not succeed in determining all of the books De Quincey claims to have consulted. The usual method employed, that of tracing De Quincey's passing allusions to books or authors, would in this case have required a disproportionate amount of labor, as De Quincey cites something like forty authors or titles in the course of his three articles—virtually a complete bibliography of everything that had been written on the Homeric question in his period.[62]

Two of the works from which De Quincey derived ideas and information, though, are Wilhelm Müller's *Homerische Vorschule, eine Einleitung in das Studium der Ilias und Odyssee* (2nd ed. Leipzig, 1836) and Robert Pashley's *Travels in Crete* (London, 1837). From Müller, whom De Quincey twice quotes directly,[63] he derived his chronological scheme of the Homeric literature, his discussion of the anachronisms in the *Iliad*, and the material on the Alexandrine Critics and their interpolations. The long and curious demonstration of Homer's Cretan origin, with the supporting quotations and other evidence, is taken over from Pashley.[64] These two books are not, however, sufficient to account for all the material in De Quincey's series. And so it must be assumed that he had other sources, probably several of them. In any case, it is clear that the articles on Homer are simply a compendium of information drawn from books of no very high scholarly standing, which De Quincey is eager to mask by his little hoax of Nitzsch and the German encyclopedia. Probably, he felt that the name of this respected German scholar would lend an air of authority to his rehash of material contained in popular or merely introductory works on the subject.

The curiously titled "Casuistry of Roman Meals"[65] has been singled out by Mr. Sackville-West as an instance of De Quincey of his very worst.[66] The paper was intended to be a piece of scholarly humor, a playful discussion of an antiquarian theme—the nature of Roman meals. De Quincey claims to have made the discovery that the Romans had only one principal meal (*coenum*), which they took late in the day, and that their breakfast (*jentaculum*) and lunch (*prandium*) were casual repasts taken amidst the business of the day and even sometimes skipped.

Although the paper as a whole is best described as a rigmarole and has no particular importance, it does strike one as odd that, despite the facetiousness of the treatment, De Quincey should be able to exhibit so much learning on this out-of-the-way subject. It would contradict the contention of this study that De Quincey's erudition was specious, if for such a casual paper as this he could summon up a considerable number of apt citations from Latin and Greek authors elucidating *jentaculum*, *prandium* and *coenum*.[67]

It is logical to assume at first that De Quincey had derived his information from some work of scholarship. Examining the essay carefully for clues to his source, one notes several allusions to Salmasius, the scholar whose edition of the *Augustan History* was used by De Quincey in writing "The Caesars." These allusions suggest what in fact is the truth—that in studying the notes (which sometimes amount to little treatises) appended to the text of the *Augustan History*, De Quincey was struck by an interesting discussion of the Roman meals. And indeed, paging through a voluminous variorum edition of the *Scriptores Historiae Augustae*, one finds an elaborate footnote by Salmasius attached to the life of Tacitus by Flavius Vopiscus that contains all those citations and bits of factual material which form the core of De Quincey's facetious article.[68] These same notes, it should be added, probably provided De Quincey with his scholarly ammunition on a number of other occasions. The use he made of them in "The Caesars"[69] has already been indicated.

Proceeding with no knowledge of De Quincey's methods,

a critic who is examining his work frontally and endeavoring to analyze it as literature and scholarship would be puzzled indeed by the obvious deficiencies of the inferior papers, which are quite numerous, and which contrast so strangely with De Quincey's best scholarship, and his brilliantly written abstracts on Bentley and Pope. Such a critic would perceive, of course, all the deficiencies which have been noted here. He would be puzzled by the omission of major points of interest; he would be disturbed by the curious concentration upon secondary issues; and he would be exasperated by the monstrous digressions, the unevenness of the style, and the many irregularities in the manner of exposition.

Now all these traits have been frequently commented on by scholars and critics.[70] They have been formularized as De Quincey's "manner," and this notorious manner has been discussed endlessly, as if it were something fundamental to De Quincey's nature—the natural manifestation of his peculiar and eccentric temperament.[71] Some critics, of course, have explained the eccentricity of De Quincey's procedure by stressing his occupation as a journalist, as though that could account for all the faults of his inferior work. But it is obvious that journalism cannot be invoked to explain bad work, when it also provided the occasion for all of De Quincey's best work. It has also been said that it was natural for a writer who produced so much to lapse occasionally from the best standards of composition and to proceed in a free and improvisatory manner. But as a writer De Quincey was always scrupulous and conscientious and exerted himself to the fullest to present his matter with deliberation and art.[72] Therefore, the usual explanations of De Quincey's failures are not satisfactory, if only because they posit conditions that apply equally to the worst and to the best of his writings.

Now this whole question of De Quincey's manner, it seems clear, is in reality a false issue. De Quincey was a writer who had to be primed before he could write. With a substantial body of information and with enough leading ideas, he could turn out any given quantity of brilliant, well-organized prose, stiffened with authority and vivid with sharply-etched detail. In his works of abridgment, one never finds him digressing or padding or running thin. He is invariably direct, concise, and solid. Can it not then be assumed that the only factor relevant in a discussion of De Quincey's virtues and vices as an expositor is the question of his source, its relative adequacy or inadequacy? How differently, one wonders, would any writer have performed when compelled, as De Quincey frequently was, to make articles out of insufficient materials? Writing under such conditions anyone would have been forced to digress, to exaggerate, and to bluff. The De Quincey manner, therefore, may best be understood as the tactics of a hard-pressed writer seeking to make the most of his opportunities, and trying desperately to mask his weakness.

3

"The Last Days of Immanuel Kant,"[73] a delightful anecdotal sketch of the great German philosopher in his declining years, is at once one of the best and one of the most anomalous of De Quincey's works. As a circumstantial account of Kant's domestic life, based on reliable German sources and presented soberly as a work of scholarship, the natural inclination is to place this composition among De Quincey's biographical writings, which in fact is where it stands in the standard edition. However, as all the circumstances and incidents seem to have been selected and developed with the intention of emphasizing the humorous incongruity between Kant's character as the foremost thinker of modern times and his queer behavior as a senile old man, the sophisticated reader is likely to assume that De Quincey has treated his material more as an artist intent on comic effects than as a biographer concerned to deliver an accurate report.

In his appreciative remarks on the "Last Days," Sackville-West endeavors to balance and even to reconcile these opposed views of De Quincey's narrative as fact and as art.

> This essay is in reality much more than the mere loosely strung together series of anecdotes which a superficial reading might announce it as being. The whole thing is in fact a very cunning résumé of the chief German authorities on the subject; but De Quincey's affection for, and knowledge of, his subject, coupled with his inspired ear for significant gossip, has produced an organic whole in which the man Kant assumes the vivid life of a character in a novel by Dickens. Yet he is true in both senses, real and artistic; and so is the material by which he is created and illustrated. Indeed, this piece is one of the best examples of De Quincey's narrative power, of his ability to relate actual facts in such a way that they assume for us the strange and comically violent definition of actions in a dream.[74]

Sackville-West is concerned to emphasize the unity of this composition because, according to De Quincey's own statement, the paper is a compilation of anecdotes from several German authorities. When it was first published in *Blackwood's Edinburgh Magazine* in 1826, "The Last Days of Immanuel Kant" bore a subscription running thus: "From the German of Wasianski, Jachmann, Borowski, and Others." But, in revising the work many years later for the collected edition, De Quincey expunged this subscription and introduced his narrative with the following phrase: "Now let us begin, premising that for the most part it is Wasianski who speaks." A superior numeral follows this phrase, and glancing down to the foot of the page, one finds the following note:

> "It is Wasianski who speaks":—*This notification, however, must not be too rigorously interpreted. Undoubtedly it would be wrong, and of evil example, to distribute*

and confound the separate responsibilities of men. When
the opinions involve important moral distinctions, by all
means let every man hang by his own hook, and answer
for no more than he has solemnly undertaken for. But,
on the other hand, it would be most annoying to the
reader if all the petty recollections of some ten or fourteen men reporting upon Kant were individually to be
labelled each with its separate certificate of origin and
ownership. Wasianski loquitur may be regarded as the
running title: but it is not, therefore, to be understood
that Wasianski is always responsible for each particular
opinion or fact reported, unless where it is liable to doubt
or controversy. In that case, the responsibility is cautiously
discriminated and restricted.

(IV, 329 n)

Like Falstaff's "men in Kendal green" De Quincey's
German authorities multiply mysteriously in the course of
his tangled and shifty explanations. At any rate, he has
dropped a clue by naming the three early biographers of
Kant—Wasianski, Jachmann, and Borowski.

Looking up the first of these, Wasianski, one finds that
his book bears the promising title *Immanuel Kant in seinen
letzten Lebensjahren: Ein Beytrag zur Kenntniss seines
Charakters und häuslichen Lebens aus dem täglichen
Umgange mit ihm* (*Immanuel Kant During the Last Years
of His Life: A Contribution to the Knowledge of His Character and Domestic Circumstances Derived from Daily
Intercourse with Him*).[75] From the introduction to this
volume one learns that Wasianski was the great philosopher's *famulus*; that he assisted him in the management
of his household; and that he was Kant's principal support
in his declining years. Wasianski was evidently embarrassed
by the revealing nature of his account, and he struggles
awkwardly through a good many pages in his introduction,
making excuses for disclosing the intimate details of his

hero's life. He concludes his apology by defining succinctly his intention: "Without paint and stripped of all pomp—in his negligee, so to speak—I shall portray a man who played a leading role on the great stage of the learned world with almost universal applause."[76]

Kant *en négligé* is a pretty good definition of De Quincey's account. And so, rather eagerly, one turns the page and reads the first sentences of Wasianski's narrative.

> My acquaintance with him did not begin during the last years of his life: and to become familiar with him required more than a decade. In the year 1773 or 1774 (I do not know exactly), I attended his lectures; and later I became his amanuensis. Through this latter connection I was in closer relations with him than any of his other students. Without my asking for it, he granted me the privilege of attending his lectures free of charge.[77]

De Quincey's narrative commences thus:

> *My knowledge of Professor Kant began long before the period to which this little memorial of him chiefly refers. In the year 1773 or 1774, I cannot exactly say which, I attended his lectures. Afterwards I acted as his amanuensis; and in that office was naturally brought into a closer connexion with him than any other of the students; so that, without any request on my part, he granted me a general privilege of free access to his classroom.*
>
> (IV, 329)

In its commencement, then, De Quincey's famous paper is nothing more than a close, literal translation of an obscure German memorialist. As he proceeds, however, De Quincey begins to free himself a little from the pedestrian movement of Wasianski's narrative, and the translation, though never deviating from the thought and sequence of the original, becomes more free in style and more spirited in temper. And soon one discovers that De Quincey has

omitted many uninteresting passages and many details that
he probably felt were simply mean and ugly. He has cut
out the reports of Kant's humiliating patience with bad
servants, his plan to give away all his money, his lack of
manual dexterity, his strange notion that daylight breeds
bugs, and his anti-English sentiments. In all, he has reduced
Wasianski's text by about one-third, and occasionally he
has rearranged the details of a particular discussion to improve the order of exposition. In some passages he has
taken great pains to elevate the rather dumpy style of the
original, and when the matter militates against De Quincey's pure and elegant language, he has brought the facts
into line with the manner. For example, according to
Wasianski, Kant's rustic pleasures were simply those of a
good German burgher:

> The country house mentioned so often already is situ-
> ated on high ground under tall alders. Below, in the
> valley, flows a little brook with a waterfall, whose rush-
> ing sound Kant noticed. This excursion awakened in him
> a dormant idea, which became extremely vivid. Subse-
> quently, Kant described for me—with an almost poetic
> pictorialness, which he generally avoided in his narrations
> —the pleasure he had received in his early years from a
> beautiful summer morning when he sat in an arbour
> (on a country estate) in an *allée* lined with lofty trees,
> drinking a cup of coffee and smoking a pipe.[78]

De Quincey converts this passage into a pretty idyll un-
disturbed by such homely articles as a cup of coffee or a
pipe of tobacco.

> *In particular, the cottage itself, standing under the
> shelter of tall alders, with a valley silent and solitary
> stretched beneath it, through which a little brook me-
> andered, broken by a waterfall, whose pealing sound
> dwelt pleasantly on the ear, sometimes on a quiet sunny
> day gave a lively delight to Kant: and once, under acci-
> dental circumstances of summer-clouds and sunlights,*

the little pastoral landscape suddenly awakened a lively
remembrance, which had been long laid asleep, of a
heavenly summer morning in youth which he had passed
in a bower upon the banks of a rivulet that ran through
the grounds of a dear and early friend.

(IV, 362–63)

By heightening the style and by cutting out the dead
wood, De Quincey has contrived greatly to improve the
appearance of Wasianski's amateurishly written report.
However, it must be stressed that this splendid paper,
which is found in all the popular anthologies of De Quincey's writings, and which has been regarded by the best of
De Quincey's critics as a highly characteristic product of
his art, is essentially a translation of a German book of
memoirs.

But, it will be asked, what of the humorous effect of
the paper? What of those deliciously comic scenes in
which a reader is impelled to burst out laughing at the
absurd spectacle of the greatest thinker of the modern
world whining after his coffee like a pettish child, swathing
himself in his bedclothes at night with ritualistic deliberate-
ness, or springing out of bed in the morning at the per-
emptory command of a boorish servant? How does one
account for the humorous design of De Quincey's paper,
if it is merely a translation of a sober and exact memoir?

The answer to all these questions is simply that Wasianski's account of Kant's last days is a classic example of
unconscious humor. By narrating the senile antics of the
great philosopher in the prosaic tones of a sympathetic
medical attendant, Wasianski frequently achieves, quite
unintentionally, an effect which is almost that of burlesque.
His naive hero worship blinded him to the absurdity of his
subject. But De Quincey's twinkling eyes were open to the
humor inherent in every grotesque detail. He saw that by
merely editing and translating the book, taking care to

heighten the most amusing moments, he would achieve an effect worthy of an original humorist.

One example will suffice to show what he was about in translating this piece: the comic description of Kant's procedure in laying himself to sleep. Wasianski has reverently preserved every detail of Kant's ritual.

> Through long practice he had acquired a special skill for swathing himself in the bedclothes. Upon retiring, he sat himself upon the bed; then, he vaulted with ease into it; next, he pulled a corner of the cover over one shoulder down and around his back to the other shoulder; then with especial adroitness, he got the opposite corner under him, and finished by wrapping the rest of the blanket about his body. So wrapped up—almost like a spun cocoon—he awaited sleep.[79]

De Quincey has realized the humor inherent in this description perfectly.

> *Long practice had taught him a very dexterous mode of nesting and enswathing himself in the bedclothes. First of all, he sat down on the bedside; then with an agile motion he vaulted obliquely into his lair; next he drew one corner of the bedclothes under his left shoulder, and, passing it below his back, brought it round so as to rest under his right shoulder; fourthly, by a particular tour d'adresse, he operated on the other corner in the same way; and finally contrived to roll it round his whole person. Thus swathed like a mummy, or (as I used to tell him) self-involved like the silk-worm in its cocoon, he awaited the approach of sleep.*

(iv, 338)

By editing Wasianski so that his account becomes a sequence of scenes such as this, De Quincey has concentrated the humorous elements in his original, and made them the central feature of the work.[80]

In all of the papers considered up to this point there

has been no instance of verbal plagiarism; and indeed, the reason must be obvious. De Quincey had no need of other men's words. Although inadequate as a scholar and a thinker, he was always a facile and brilliant writer. It was matter he required, not language. And so almost all of his borrowings consist in appropriations of bodies of facts and opinions, the language in every case being his own.

There are, however, two instances in addition to the "Last Days" in which he has simply translated a foreign work and published it as his own, merely making certain editorial revisions so as to adapt what was originally a book or treatise to the form of a magazine article. In both of these cases his originals are just as obscure as Wasianski's book on Kant; and doubtless he relied upon their obscurity as insurance against detection. It must also be observed that in each instance he makes some amends for what he is doing by contriving to mention the author without betraying the fact of plagiarism.

"The Toilette of the Hebrew Lady,"[81] an elaborate description of the historical costume of Hebrew women in Biblical times, was based, according to De Quincey's own statement,[82] upon an obscure German treatise, *Die Hebräerin am Putztische und als Braut* by Ernst Hartmann, published in Amsterdam in the year 1809. This huge dissertation—still the standard work on the subject and a very rare book—De Quincey claims to have drastically abridged to one-twenty-eighth of its original size without the loss of essential matter. This preposterous claim is found amidst a long series of facetious and disparaging remarks upon Herr Hartmann, whose book De Quincey describes as a hopelessly muddled and typically German production.[83] De Quincey is forever disparaging the German scholars upon whom he was so dependent, and, as one would suspect, his accusations are largely without basis.

Mr. Erhart H. Essig, in an unpublished doctoral dissertation,[84] has examined this paper in conjunction with its source and has demonstrated that, far from being an abridgment of the entire work, it is merely a translation, with judicious deletions, of a single chapter in the first volume. As this paper has already been discussed in detail by Mr. Essig,[85] it is worth remarking only upon the peculiarity of De Quincey's writing to Hogg, the editor of the collected edition of his works that "considering its *Biblical* relations, over and above its interest of curiosity, I really think this Hebrew Toilette—*with the exception always of some six or seven*—the best in the collection."[86] A remark of this sort goes far, one feels, in suggesting the complex psychological basis for De Quincey's peculiar practices of appropriation. A scheming journalist could not have had such delusions; they are rather more reminiscent of the earnest assertions of Coleridge that material he had manifestly plagiarized was really the product of his own mind.[87]

Another example of an unacknowledged translation is the "Historico-Critical Inquiry into the origin of the Rosicrucians and the Free-masons."[88] This curious paper De Quincey has explicitly labelled as an abstract, though he claimed for it, the advantage of an organization superior to that of the original, as well as other unspecified improvements. "I have therefore abstracted, rearranged, and in some respects, I shall not scruple to say, have improved, the German work on this subject, of Professor J. G. Buhle." (XIII, 385)

As usual, De Quincey's claims are somewhat in excess of his actual performance. Mr. Essig has demonstrated that his method in this paper consists in summarizing the topical portions of each paragraph, translating the key sentences literally, and omitting the voluminous supporting materials.[89] Generally, De Quincey has closely followed Buhle's arrangement of the subject; but in the latter portion of his paper he has slightly altered the order of the original to improve its sequence.

One gets a good idea of De Quincey's rationale for such

labors as these from the note he appended to this paper in the collected edition.

> *It was a paper in this sense mine, that from me it had received form and arrangement; but the materials belonged to the learned German—viz. Buhle. . . . No German has any conception of style. I therefore did him the favour to wash his dirty face, and make him presentable amongst Christians; but the substance was drawn entirely from this German book.*
>
> (VII, 201–2)

Although most of De Quincey's papers on scholarly subjects have gone unchallenged as products of independent research, two papers have been suspected as plagiarisms. In both cases, oddly enough, the works are probably original; the difficulty has arisen from an improper understanding of De Quincey's productive processes. Works of real learning he evidently could not produce, because his preparation was inadequate. But an analysis, or an exegetical commentary upon a single book, anything, in short, that required only intelligence and not a collection of materials, he was certainly capable of writing without aid.

Professor Oliver Elton has stated (without, however, advancing any evidence to substantiate his assertions) that "[De Quincey] was capable of taking some dull or remote authority, saying nothing about it, and dressing it out, without scruple, for the readers of his journal."[90] This, as has been seen, is a substantially accurate description of De Quincey's procedure in a great many articles. However, Mr. Elton instances as proof only the series of papers on the Essenes,[91] which, the author of the present study is persuaded, is one of the few exceptions to the rule. Possibly it was the esoteric nature of the subject that aroused the suspicions of Professor Elton. This in itself, though, is of no significance, for it is the nature of De Quincey's undertaking rather than the character of his subject that is decisive in these questions of plagiarism.

The papers on the Essenes are merely eccentric speculations based upon a study of a few passages in Josephus' *History of the Jews*, readily accessible to De Quincey in the English translation of William Whiston.[92] From the few notices of the Essenes in Josephus, De Quincey elaborated a very ambitious hypothesis consisting of two principal assertions: first, that the Essenes considered as a Hebrew sect were really an invention of Josephus designed to discredit Christianity by depriving it of its claim to originality; and second, that the Essenes were in fact the primitive Christians attempting to protect themselves by the assumption of another name.

The very unsoundness of this hypothesis suggests its originality. For had De Quincey, according to his usual practice, consulted the German authorities of his day he would have found a much different presentation of the matter. The principal German work of the time was Johann Joachim Bellermann's *Geschichtliche Nachrichten aus dem Alterthume über Essäer und Therapeuten* (Berlin, 1821). Herr Bellermann, like any real student of this subject, derives his information from all the ancient authorities, not just from Josephus; and he also considers the traditional lore of the Talmud and the Jewish Rabbis. His conclusions are substantially in accord with modern findings, for he establishes on the one hand the similarities between the Essenes and the primitive Christians, and, on the other, their differences and their historical individuality. The great difference between an authentic work of scholarship on this question and De Quincey's arguments is that the scholar surveys all the evidence and deduces appropriate conclusions; whereas De Quincey constructs his hypothesis upon a much narrower base and extends it by forcing the evidence to a predetermined result. De Quincey's commitment to Christianity was so doctrinaire that he could not admit the existence in the Hebrew world of a sect whose doctrines so clearly anticipated those of Christianity. It is characteristic of his total want of real learning that he should endeavor to draw a hard and fast line between Christianity and the religious sects that preceded it.

Professor René Wellek suspects plagiarism in De Quincey's analysis of Kant's *Kritik der reinen Vernunft*, contained in the paper entitled in the Masson edition *German Studies and Kant in Particular*.[93] This paper is actually part of De Quincey's autobiographical reminiscences. He describes the passionate desire he had as a student at Oxford to penetrate the mysteries of the Kantian philosophy and his subsequent disillusionment when he discovered the "negative" or purely critical character of this philosophy. In the midst of his reminiscence he embarks upon an extended analysis of the central tenets of the *Critique*, starting with the problem of causality as it was defined by Hume, and from this point, developing Kant's ideas as an answer to Hume's skeptical conclusions.

There is undoubtedly a disparity between De Quincey's language and attitude in the passages that precede and follow the analysis of Kant and the language and attitude he adopts in the analysis itself. For example, in the introduction to his analysis, De Quincey characterizes Kant's conclusions as "negative"; yet in the analysis itself he contrasts the "positive" doctrines of Kant with the purely "negative" philosophy of Locke. Upon this and certain other disparities Professor Wellek fastens and writes as follows: "This juxtaposition of irreconcilable statements leads us to conjecture that [De Quincey's] correct formulas were taken from some German exposition without any clear comprehension of their interconnection and consequences."[94]

As the disparities Professor Wellek has noted might well be evidence of plagiarism, the author of the present study examined very carefully the early German commentators

on Kant; but found nothing to corroborate the suggestion.
He was about to give up, when he accidentally encountered
a passage in another paper of De Quincey's, published
several years before the one on Kant, which greatly clari-
fied the whole question. The paper is "Recollections of
Hannah More," and the pertinent passage runs as follows:

> As to myself, knowing that I was a philosophical student,
> she so far did violence to her own tastes . . . as twice to
> seek my aid in metaphysical embarrassments. Once was
> with respect to the philosophic scheme of Immanuel
> Kant: without minute details, she wished for a general
> rude outline of its purposes and its machinery. The other
> case regarded the Humian doctrine of cause and effect.
> . . . I succeeded in realizing the old proverb and killing
> two birds with one stone; for I so dovetailed the two
> answers together that the explanation of Kant was made
> to arise naturally and easily out of the mere statement
> of Hume's problem on the idea of necessary connexion.
> . . . My answer, though short indeed for so vast a sub-
> ject, was however, too long to be inserted in this place.
> Probably I shall publish it in a separate form.

(XIV, 126–27)

Since it was De Quincey's habit to carry about with him
notes and papers that might serve as a basis for future
articles, it may be assumed that the analysis of Kant he
describes in the above passage with such obvious pride is
the very same analysis that disturbed Professor Wellek.
Evidently, in writing of his youthful disillusionment with
the Kantian philosophy, De Quincey saw an opportunity
for introducing the scrap which he had long been saving
for just such an occasion; but as the analysis of Kant had
been written years before with an entirely different purpose
in view, there inevitably arose a difficulty in splicing it
into the current context. This difficulty De Quincey did

not successfully circumvent, but there is no reason now to doubt that the exposition is original.[95]

This matter is clearly of some importance, not only because it vindicates De Quincey from a charge of plagiarism in this, his only extended treatment of Kant, but also because it confirms a general rule that the research of the present study has established—namely, that in any matter requiring merely intellectual ability De Quincey is not likely to have plagiarized; but when it is a question of special knowledge, facts and ideas that can only be obtained by thorough research, then in almost every instance he is dependent on a single source.

Rifacimento

AS A SCHOLAR, De Quincey was so ill-equipped that he was forced to rifle the writings of more learned authors in order to obtain the information and ideas necessary for his purposes. However, as modern criticism has noted, the essential strength of De Quincey's mind was not his intellectual capacites and attainments, but rather his power of imagination and his purely literary gifts.

Although some of the papers that this study will now consider nominally belong to the categories of biography, history, and scholarship, they are, by and large, writings distinguished by imaginative qualities—by vivid characterization, suggestive description, and skillful narrative.

The best of these papers take their place among De Quincey's finest achievements. Like the *Confessions*, the "Suspiria" and the other original works of self-portraiture and fantasy, these papers—which include the "Revolt of the Tartars," the "Postscript" to "On Murder Considered as One of the Fine Arts," and "The Spanish Military Nun" —possess the qualities of impassioned prose and poetic imagination that are De Quincey's principal virtues. Of course, the fact that these compositions are derived from printed sources does not, from the literary point of view, make them any less original; and simply to have revealed the fact of their derivation is not in itself a very important achievement. What is important is the opportunity they afford to study, in the most exact way, the workings of De

Quincey's imagination, which always have a certain con-
sistency, whether acting on the stuff of his experience,
dreams, and fantasies or whether assimilating and transforming such literary materials as memoirs, books, newspaper reports, and personal documents. The same imaginative processes that produced the most admired pages of the
Confessions are evident in the "Revolt of the Tartars" and
the "Postscript." In the case of these latter papers, however, it is possible to go behind the finished composition
and study the process by which it was produced, as it is
not possible to do with the *Confessions*. The literary and
imaginative processes by which De Quincey produced his
works, at least those that allow themselves to be studied in
conjunction with a source, constitute so consistent a technique that, once familiar with it, one can infer pretty
accurately what De Quincey did with his source to produce
his work. To be sure, from a study such as this, one cannot
determine exactly what is genuine and what is invented in
such a book as the *Confessions*; but, if so inclined, one can
make some shrewd guesses.

1

On April 28, 1841, De Quincey sent a new article
to his publisher, Robert Blackwood, with a covering note
explaining that the composition was an "Abstract from the
Memoirs of Arndt;" that it was to be titled, "Russia in the
Summer and Winter of 1812;" and that it contained passages from Arndt "equal to any in the *Plague of Athens* as
reported by Thucydides."[1] Having become sufficiently
familiar with De Quincey's practices, one is hardly sur-
prised to learn that these remarks misrepresent the relation
between his article and its source.

The so-called "abstract" is not, as De Quincey describes
it more fully in his introduction, "woven together from
scattered pages of Arndt," but is rather a consecutive,

though very free, translation of one small section of Arndt's book, *Erinnerungen aus dem Äusseren Leben* (1840). As for the passages "equal to any in the *Plague of Athens*," these, as shall be seen, are not to be found in Arndt; they were all written by De Quincey himself.

In presenting his selection from the *Recollections* of Ernst Moritz Arndt, De Quincey undoubtedly was counting upon the fame of the German patriot and poet to command the interest of his English readers. Arndt had been the most popular spokesman for German independence and liberty during the period of Napoleonic tyranny,[2] and, as an active and courageous patriot, he had participated, at least as an observer, in some of the momentous events of the Napoleonic Wars. In the section of the *Recollections* that De Quincey used as the basis for his paper, for example, Arndt describes a journey he took in the summer of 1812 from Vienna to Moscow and St. Petersburg and back again the following winter from St. Petersburg to Königsberg in East Prussia. In the course of this journey, Arndt observed both the vast preparations to repel the Napoleonic invasion and the terrible devastation left in the wake of the retreating French armies. All this should make fascinating reading; but, as a matter of fact, in the thin and sketchy prose of the *Recollections* the extraordinary scenes Arndt had witnessed seem very dim and remote. There is neither the vividness of an immediate report nor the thoroughness of a good literary memoir.

De Quincey was undoubtedly aware of these inadequacies in Arndt's account, and sought to remedy the situation by substituting his own lively prose for the feeble style of the original and by filling in the sketchy outlines of Arndt's narrative with an abundance of detail from his own imagination. The alteration in style is evident when one compares such a passage as the following with De Quincey's heightened version of the same.

I saw here [in Smolensk], among a host of various and shifting figures, the different Russian ethnic groups as they marched or galloped past me, men from the Polar Sea and the Urals, men who water their horses in the Volga and the Black Sea, handsome Tartars from the Kabarda and the Crimea, stately Cossacks from the Don, Kalmucks with flat noses, wooden bodies, crooked legs, and slanted eyes (just as Ammianus depicts his Huns 1500 years ago), and Bashkirs with bows and arrows. The most splendid sight, however, was a single squadron, from a troop of Circassian cavalry, wearing chain mail and steel helmets with fluttering plumes, handsome, slender men and fine horses.[3]

Now here is De Quincey's version:

Continually in this week at Smolensko, streaming through the streets, but to more advantage as approaching along the roads from Moscow or St. Petersburg, one would see the pompous array of armies under every variety and modification that Europe or Asia can furnish. Now came, for hours together, the sealike tread of infantry, the main masses of modern warfare, the marching regiments of the Czar's armies. Then, after an interval of ten minutes, would be heard the thunder of cavalry approaching; and immediately began to fly past us, like a hurricane, squadrons after squadrons of those whose horses had drunk from the Wolga or the Caspian; many with Siberian fur barretts, who lived near the icy ocean; fine races of Tartars from the Kabarda and the Crimea; men from three different sides of the Euxine, and both side of the Ural Mountains; stately Cossacks from the Don; Kalmucks, with flat noses, and bodies square and wooden legs, and eyes set obliquely, precisely as Ammianus Marcellinus describes the Huns of Attila's armies fifteen centuries ago; Hulans careering with vast spears; Chinese-looking men from the pastoral Tartars of the great eastern steppes; and ugly Bashkirs, with blinking malicious eyes, and

> armed, even in this era of civilization, [hear it, Captain
> Dalgetty!] with bows, and sounding arrow-sheafs rattling
> on their backs. But, perhaps, the most interesting (cer-
> tainly the most beautiful) interlude in this prodigious
> mask of martial life was, whenever a squadron of Cir-
> cassian cavalry cantered past; all of them in glittering steel
> shirts of mail, all carrying floating plumes of the most
> beautiful description in their helmets, all superbly
> mounted, men and horses alike presenting the same tall,
> graceful, slender figures and features, contrasting so
> powerfully with the quadrangular massy bodies and side-
> long leer of the ugly Kalmucks and Bashkirs.[4]

Although De Quincey has added here nothing essential,
he has improved the original text at every point. He has
realized the suggestion of large masses of men in motion
("vorbeimarschiren," "vorbeigalloppiren") by evoking the
steady rhythm of tramping infantry followed by the swift
flight of cavalry. And, similarly, he has amplified and inten-
sified the imagery and improved its arrangement to bring out
effectively, at the close for example, the contrast between
the graceful Circassian horsemen and the awkward figures
of the Kalmucks and Bashkirs.

The basic fabric of De Quincey's paper is just this sort of
free translation—rewriting, heightening, rearranging. However, rewriting alone was not adequate to realize all those
suggestions for a more impressive kind of presentation that
De Quincey found scattered throughout his text. And so at
every opening for a more ample treament, he had introduced his own realization of the theme. When Arndt in his
hasty style sketches the ruins of the Russian villages, for
example, De Quincey substitutes for the sketch a detailed
and vivid picture.

> Many torn, smashed, unroofed houses without people or
> animals—not even a cat was mewing inside; hideously
> desolate walls and ruins.[5]

every where roofless houses, with not so much as a cat
mewing amongst the ruins; shapeless wrecks where there
had been villages or churches; heaps of forlorn chimneys,
stone window-frames or mullions, rafters scorched and
blackened; oftentimes piles of nondescript rubbish, from
which rose up through melting snow smouldering flames,
vapours, and a hideous odor, that too often bespoke the
secret crimes lurking below—bodies rotting and slowly
burning, probably those of unoffending peasants.[6]

There are other passages (of a length that forbids quotation) in which De Quincey thoroughly reimagines from a
few indications in his source scenes and events of the utmost horror. There is, for example, a minute and poring
description of the sick and wounded French prisoners,
packed under "the iron rigour of frost."[7] In all of these passages one detects De Quincey's impatience with his self-
imposed task of improving upon his German original. One
is also conscious of a tendency to break away from Arndt's
prosaic report, and to be off upon a freer flight of imagination. At only one point in this paper, however, does he
totally transcend the character of his material, and even in
this splendid passage he is controlled, at least in his direction, by the text which he is rendering. Still, the extreme
incongruity between De Quincey's inspired Romanticism
and the perfunctoriness of Arndt is startlingly evident when
the two passages are juxtaposed. Arndt is describing the
impressions of an afternoon spent in the country outside
Smolensk.

I had gone outside the city and had stretched myself
behind a haystack in a green meadow where quiet herds
were grazing as if there were no war; a thick-leaved birch
fluttered above my head. Thoughtfully, dreamily I contemplated the world at large, or, rather, I gazed at the
clouds flowing over me. Behold! Then music sounded in
my ears! The sound became more distinct as it drew
closer. Soon long trains of wagons rolled past bearing

militiamen with their parents, brothers and sisters, and brides—the whole preceded by fiddles and pipes. Thus merrily, with flowers and music, they marched off to war and death, appearing to the pensive observer like a vision of a wedding in a dream.[8]

Such a visionary appearance could not fail to arouse De Quincey's imagination. Here is his realization of the experience.

One day, finding myself perfectly wearied and exhausted by the never-ending successions of troops streaming onwards to the west, I moved round the skirts of the town, until I reached a situation so distant from the great tumult, that no sound could be caught even of trumpets and kettle-drums; the roar of baggage-waggons died away on the wind, the groaning of heavy artillery oppressed the ear no longer. It was noonday—sultry as usual; and that peculiar silence, so breathless, solemn and Pan-like, which sometimes belongs to the deep noon, whether of day or night, disposed even the thoughtless man to reverie. I had flung myself upon a soft, lawny couch of heathy ground: no one moving object was in sight; indeed, no living creature whatever, except some peaceful cattle tranquilly reposing under the shade of umbrageous trees half a mile distant. Solemn forests could be seen skirting the backgrounds in one direction; and the eye could dimly penetrate the gloomy recesses which their openings revealed. The imagination peopled these awe-inspiring solitudes with corresponding inhabitants; but to the mere bodily eye, all was silent, motionless, breathless, as the grave. Such being the external scene, it was inevitable that one's thoughts should revert to the tremendous scenes of havoc, struggle, and carnal fury, just now in the very crisis of opening. Then came the antagonist thought presenting the utter stillness, the inaudible tread, of that final grave which was so surely stealing onwards to swallow up, in one common abyss of darkness, the horse and his rider,

the master and the slave, the mover of this mighty up-
roar, and the poor sutler that dogged his heels for bread.
Five-and-twenty or thirty years hence, thought I, say in
the year 1840 what will have become of these innumer-
able captains, marshals, plumed cavaliers so stately and
exulting? The earth shakes beneath their sounding tread
on this day of August 1812. But if the curtain of time
could draw up on the sad wrecks of these brilliant armies
as they will exist one generation a-head; if—but just at
that moment rose a solemn breathing of wind from the
forests, so sad, so full of woe in its sound, half between a
sigh and a groan, that I was really startled, as if mute
nature had understood and answered my ejaculation. It
was a sound, beyond all I ever heard, that expressed a
requiem and a lamentation over the pomps and glories of
man—so noble in his aspirations, so full of beauty and
power for the moment—yet so inevitably lying down,
after one generation, in dust and ashes, that I sank even
deeper into abstractions gloomy and full of tears.

What was it that wakened me? You have seen, reader,
those pictures called "Dances of Death," where the mar-
rowless and eyeless skeleton, which typifies the "meagre
shadow," is represented as linked in festal dances (though
masked to their eyes) with the forms of crowned kings,
mailed warriors, blooming brides, and rosy children. Such,
or even more fantastic, when viewed from the station of
my immediate thoughts on the vanity of vanities that
closed up the rear of these warlike prospects, was the
scene which suddenly rose up from a valley on one side,
which continued to crown, in endless succession, the
summit of the nearest hill, and thence diffused itself like
a deluge over the unenclosed declivity reaching to the
suburbs. Rustic waggons by thousands, as if for some vast
festival of early vintagers, all decorated with flowers and
verdant ferns, came on with haste, bringing along a whole
army of the local militia, or armed populace of the rural

districts, from territories far inland. Militia, strictly speaking, they were not; for they had been embodied only to
meet the immediate purpose of harassing the French rear
or lateral detachments. They were, therefore, something
like our Prussian landwehr in constitution; but far different were the circumstances attending their motions
towards the general rendezvous. With the men, oftentimes boys, who composed the armament, came also their
mothers, aunts, sometimes grandmothers, sisters, sweet-
hearts; in short, six armies of women and girls for one of
men. Hence the flowers; hence the music, floating from
every portable instrument that the earth has ever known;
hence the laughter, the shouting, the jubilation;—like
some fantastic bridal in fairyland, "a sight to dream of,
not to tell," and even for dreams too like delirium or
frenzy.

Was this wild mockery of care and forethought the
proper sequel to my solemn reveries? I leaped up from
the ground; unprofitable sorrow vanished; and I was soon
myself as much carried off my feet by the contagion of
the patriotic rejoicing which accompanied their encamp-
ment on the hillsides, as the most thoughtless of the
boys.[9]

This astonishing flight will bear comparison with all but
the very best of De Quincey's "original" writing. It has the
same wonderful freedom of movement, the same rich sug-
gestiveness of description, and the same melancholy tone
as the *Confessions* or the dream-fantasies. And, as in these
works, the reader is especially affected by those magical
alternations of mood which characterize equally the progress
of the great Romantic odes—such as those of Wordsworth,
Shelley, and Keats—and the form of the finest Romantic
music—the sonatas and symphonies of Beethoven and Schu-
bert.

It soon becomes evident that everything of literary value

contained in this paper is a result of De Quincey's own efforts to transform and to improve his material. To be sure, he has made no real attempt to assimilate the material or, by infusing it with a new theme, to shape it into a work of genuine originality. He has consistently followed the outline of his source and merely endeavored to raise its style and realize its potentialities for the picturesque. Yet the tendency of his efforts is evident; and from even such a modest example of his art as this, one can understand the essential nature of his imaginative processes. These are especially characterized by a tendency toward the pictorial; and, in the other papers to be discussed, many, and more elaborate, examples of this impressive mode of visualization will be found.

It is, of course, ironic that De Quincey, who on so many other occasions illicitly appropriated the ideas and information of other men, should now be discovered in the act of tranferring his own imaginative productions to an author quite unequal to them. However, one must bear in mind, as always, the peculiar conditions under which he worked. A presentation of materials gleaned from the actual memoirs of a famous public figure would, from the journalistic point of view, be of far greater value than any fictionalized version of the same material proceeding from the pen of the English Opium Eater. It was truth, although truth of imaginative proportions, that De Quincey always maintained he was offering to his magazine readers. A story that could not claim the sanction of history would for them, he felt, have no real value; but, of course, an honest translation of Arndt's feeble narrative would have failed as literature; and so, caught between these contending demands, De Quincey was compelled to efface himself as a creative spirit.

The kind of rewriting, rearranging, and reimagining which one finds in De Quincey's treatment of Arndt, and occasionally, to a lesser degree, in his translation of Wasianski, is closely related to, if not identical with, the practice known as *rifacimento*. As this was one of De Quincey's basic techniques as an imaginative author, one might expect to find some reference to it, perhaps a defense of it, in his critical writings. Yet the word never once appears in any of the papers reprinted in the standard edition of his works. Such a discussion is to be found, though, in a long and interesting review, never reprinted, of his friend Robert Pearse Gillies' *German Stories.*[10] This review is a *locus criticus* for the study of De Quincey's art and literary criticism; and it is surprising to observe that Professor Jordan, in his admirable treatment of De Quincey as a critic, makes no reference to the Gillies review.

Of several passages dealing with *rifacimento*, a technique that Gillies advocated for translations from the German, the following is perhaps the most explicit:

> Considering also how much there is in German novel-writing of what is only partially good, let us call the attention of translators to the necessity of applying, on a much larger scale, that principle of adaptation, rifacimento, or remaniement, which Mr Gillies has so repeatedly suggested. Why, let us ask, has this been so timidly practised? From a complete misconception, as we take it, of the duties of a translator of novels,—and under the very same servile conceit of fidelity which, combined with laziness and dyspepsy, has so often led translators to degrade themselves into mere echoes of the idiom and turn of sentence in the original. . . . But shall I not stick to my author? Is it lawful for me to swerve from a German Professor's novel?—Undoubtedly it is: be faithful to the Professor, where you cannot improve his plot, or inspirit his characters: wherever you can, betray the Professor— betray him into a general popularity in England, and the Professor will be the first man to send you a gold snuff-box for so doing. . . . Give us what we seek, and we ask

no questions about the proportions in which author and
translator have contributed to that result.[11]

The rather heated tone of this passage is no doubt explained by the fact that shortly before it was written De
Quincey himself was engaged—with what success will pres-
ently be seen—in "betraying" a German Professor and his
novel "into a general popularity in England."

Walladmor was the title of a novel that appeared in Germany in the year 1824 bearing the subscription "Freely
translated from the English of Walter Scott."[12] The book,
of course, was a hoax, an impudent attempt to capitalize
upon the tremendous interest that had been aroused in Germany by the Waverley Novels. The annual appearance of a
new book in this series had become an eagerly anticipated
event on the German literary calendar; and when the book-
sellers, who foregathered every year at the great book fair in
Leipzig, realized that no new novel of Scott's could appear
in their catalogue for the year 1824, they took the shortest
way to remedy the deficiency—they commissioned a German author of historical romances to write a novel which
could be passed as a translation of a new book by the
author of *Waverley*. Or so at least the story goes according
to the version of De Quincey,[13] who came to figure in this
preposterous affair by first reviewing and then translating
the fraudulent fiction. An entirely different account, however, was given by Willibald Alexis, the German hoaxer who
wrote the novel, in his *Erinnerungen*.[14] Alexis, whose real
name was Haering (*alex* is the Latin for herring), maintains
that the novel grew spontaneously out of his involvement
with Scott, whom he greatly admired and several of whose
works he had translated; that it was intended as a light-
hearted parody of Scott's manner—his complicated and im-
probable plots, his eccentric characters, and his antiquarian
preoccupations; and that no serious attempt was made to
deceive the German reading public. But it is very hard to

take the German author at his word; for although the novel is a foolish enough production, its particular quality of nonsense can hardly be ascribed to deliberate intention to parody.

Modelled upon *Guy Mannering*, the story concerns the adventures of Bertram, a young German lover of the picturesque, who, on a journey to England, is shipwrecked off the coast of Wales and rescued by some local smugglers. This motley crew includes a demented old woman of the breed of Meg Merrilies, a salty ship captain, patterned after Dirk Hatteraick, and Nicholas, a dark and mysterious counter-hero, something like the protagonist of Schiller's *The Robbers*. This character is not much in the manner of Sir Walter Scott; but he is a stock figure in the German romances of the day. Young Bertram is soon drawn into a series of adventures in which the mysterious Nicholas seeks to win back the love of Genovieve, niece to the Baron of the district, Sir Morgan Walladmor. This afflicted man has been seeking for twenty years through the arts of astrology to determine the fate of his son, who was abducted at birth. Bertram no sooner sees the fair young Genovieve than he falls in love with her and thus comes into conflict with Nicholas, to whom he is deeply obligated, as he eventually learns, for saving his life when he was shipwrecked. The conventional happy ending is achieved with some straining of probability. Nicholas is revealed as the missing son of the Baron; but, since he is an outlaw, he cannot be heir to Walladmor. And so the Baron's estate is settled upon the two lovers, Genovieve and Bertram, who are united with the blessings of Nicholas.

Recounting his adventures with this German hoax in the amusing article he published many years after the event, De Quincey portrayed himself as a man consciously participating in a farce. But the letters and records which survive from that time indicate rather that he was seeking earnestly enough to make a journalistic coup. Apparently, he had received word of the book from his old friend Bohn, the principal German bookseller in London. With his eye fixed keenly on the expected "scoop," he writes to his publisher:

> For the "bonne bouche," or 5th and last art., we must have "Walladmor" (that is ye name in the Leipzig Catal.), if Heaven or Earth can get it. An abstract of the novel, which I will make in 24 hours, will be of universal interest from the circumstances.—Pray send if you can to Bohn's. They have promised to lend Sir W. Scott's copy in default of any other, on condition of a speedy return. And within 36 hours from receiving it at most I will pledge my word for returning it. What I fear is that the copy should be snapped up by somebody on the spot.[15]

De Quincey was as good as his word. Unwilling to spoil "Sir W. Scott's" copy by cutting all the leaves, he managed nevertheless to read the book in the attitude of a man "looking up a chimney;" and in forty-eight hours he had written a delightful thirty-page review explaining the circumstances of the hoax and including long extracts ably translated, tied together by a running summary and rattling fire of sarcastic comments.[16] Unfortunately, he did his work too well. The universal interest that he anticipated actually developed and made Taylor and Hessey eager to publish a complete translation, and De Quincey got the job. It was one thing to lift out the best passages and make fun of the German author, with his impossible notions of Welsh geography and manners and his foolishly melodramatic story. But now the tables were turned, and De Quincey was committed to producing a readable version of this German rigmarole. Here is a glimpse of him at his work. "Mr. Knight describes a visit which he had paid to De Quincey at his lodging, whilst he was in the toils with 'Walladmor,' and we have this reminiscence:—'I saw him groaning over his uncongenial labour, by which he eventually got very little. It was projected to appear in three volumes. He despairingly wrote to me, "After weeding out the forests of rubbish, I believe it will make only one decent volume." ' "[17]

De Quincey was not the only man, though, to suffer from the German's audacity. Sir Walter Scott was himself alarmed by the publication of *Walladmor*, according to Lockhart:

> in 1825 Scott was about to publish *The Talisman*, his preceding novel *The Betrothed* having been put aside after all but the last chapters had been printed. Sir Walter found it impossible to write these concluding chapters, and so the sheets of all the rest of the novel were hung up in Ballantyne's warehouse. When the news came from Germany that a new novel was announced by the author of *Waverley*, Scott feared that his sheets had been pirated, and rushed to complete *The Betrothed*, which is set like *Walladmor* in Wales.[18]

De Quincey's version of *Walladmor* appeared in 1825, the three substantial volumes of the original having shrunk to two small octavos.[19] On the title-page appeared an amusingly symmetrical subscription: " 'Freely translated into German from the English of Walter Scott' and now Freely Translated From the German into the English." In his introduction De Quincey again explains the circumstances of the hoax, rallies the German author for the obvious anachronisms in his tale, and intimates that the English translator has found it necessary at times to touch up the dialogue and to rectify the mistakes in topography. But De Quincey does not say what was really the case— that he had recast the original to such an extent that it had become quite another book. Actually, he could not claim the credit that was his. He had worked himself into an impossible situation, similar in kind to the circumstances in which he had produced the abstract from Arndt. Having aroused the expectations of his publishers and the public by a somewhat too favorable representation in his review, he could not now confess that the book in which he had interested everyone was really such trash that he had been forced to rewrite it. Having exposed *Walladmor* as "the most daring hoax of the century," he could not now admit that his English translation was yet another hoax.

Aside from the dozen excerpts that De Quincey took from his review, there is practically nothing of the original in this so-called translation. The plot has been changed so that Nicholas, the sinister outlaw of the original, has now become a wholly sympathetic character—in fact, the hero of the piece. The catastrophe is entirely different, and the novel comes to a tragic close. The descriptions of the Welsh countryside as well as the local customs and manners have been replaced by material that is authentic and much more stimulating to the imagination. Needless to say, the style —and hence the tone—of the narrative has been greatly altered, the whole being written in De Quincey's best manner.

The novel which emerges from these exhaustive revisions is an attractive little romance that is rather a tour de force considering the inhibiting conditions, the necessity for holding with some of the original plot, the original cast— though not their characterizations—and the locale, which was not really familiar territory to De Quincey. The principal interest of the book derives from its scenic effects, for, as always, De Quincey has conceived his story not so much as a narrative of events, or a study of characters, but as a sequence of romantic tableaux, elaborately put together in the manner of theatrical scenery. Thus, upon a casual suggestion in the original text of a winter landscape contemplated by the hero, who is cruising along the Welsh coast, De Quincey summons up a panorama that perhaps owes more to his experience in the Lake District than to any actual observation of the Welsh coast.

The passage in the original runs as follows:

As the young man glimpsed the castle more and more clearly, as the cheerful morning sun illuminated the bright red roofs, sending its rays into the fields behind the castle—winter meadows now glowing with friendly light—he experienced an indescribable sensation of longing; and the desire to land here outweighed all his doubts.[20]

And now De Quincey's evocation of the scene.

Bertram was more and more fascinated by the aspect of the ancient castle and the quiet hills behind it, with their silent fields and woodlands, which lay basking as it were in the morning sun. The whole scene was at once gay and tranquil. The sea had put off its terrors and wore the beauty of a lake: the air was "frosty but kindly": and the shores of merry England, which he now for the first time contemplated in peace and serenity, were dressed in morning smiles; a morning, it is true, of winter; yet of winter not angry—not churlish and chiding—but of winter cheerful and proclaiming welcome to Christmas. The colours, which predominated, were of autumnal warmth: the tawny ferns had not been drenched and discoloured by rains; the oaks retained their dying leaves: and, even where the scene was most wintry, it was cheerful: the forest of pointed lances, which the deciduous trees presented, were broken pleasingly by the dark glittering leaves of the holly; and the mossy gloom of the yew and other evergreens was pierced and irradiated by the scarlet berries of various shrubs, or by the puce-coloured branches and the silvery stem of the birch.[21]

A different problem was posed by a skimpy sarcastic description of the Welsh St. David's Day procession. Scott had established a high standard of antiquarian accuracy in the representation of ancient customs and solemnities. Evidently De Quincey felt himself obliged not only to heighten the dignity and to elaborate the detail of the following description, but also to fabricate it from authentic materials.

> Amidst frequent shouts of approval from the spectators, a party of riders finally neared the inn; all of them were in step, moving as slowly and solemnly as possible. At their head rode two pairs of men, whom we shall call weapon-bearers; although a stranger might have a suspicion they were nothing more than dressed-up stable boys or servants. They wore black jockey coats, narrow leather breeches, big posting boots, and on their little hats, leafy twigs.[22]

After poring over an old book of Welsh antiquities— *Ap Howel De Lege Pricipal. per Forestam et Chasam Snowd.* (Ap Howel on the Principal Laws of the Forest and Glades of the District of Snowden)[23] De Quincey was able to mount his procession in a far more impressive style.

> *First came the Snowden archers, two and two, in their ancient uniform of green and white, in number one hundred and twenty. Immediately behind them rode a young man in black and crimson, usually called Golden-Spear from the circumstance of his carrying the gilt spear of Harlech Castle, with which, by the custom, he is to ride into Machynleth church at a certain part of the service on St. David's day, and into Dolgelly church on the day of Pentecost, and there to strike three times against 'Traitors' Grave' with a certain form of adjuration in three languages. After him came the rangers of Penmorfa, all mounted, and riding four abreast. They were in number about eighty-four; and wore, as usual, a uniform of watchet (i.e., azure) and white—with horse-cloths and housings of the same colours:—and the ancient custom had been that all the horses should be white.[24]*

Despite De Quincey's evident anxiety to impress his readers, his description easily holds its own with comparable passages on Scott.

Perhaps the finest achievement of picturesque description

in the novel is De Quincey's rewriting of a little scene in which the hero is brought within the gates of Walladmor Castle. The original contains a very slight suggestion of the *mise en scène*:

> meanwhile the bolts and bars were soon drawn; the gate went up; and the riders galloped through the arched gateway into a small courtyard illuminated by the lanterns of some old servants who had hastened there.[25]

De Quincey elaborated this passage to a grand military entrance into the vast spaces of a castle that could exist only in the imagination of a Romantic:

> *Soon after was heard the clank of bars and the creaking of the gates,*
>
> .   .   .   .
>
> *They were like the gates of a cathedral, and they began slowly to swing backward on their hinges. As they opened, the dimensions and outlines of their huge valves were defined by the light within; and, when they were fully open, a beautiful spectacle was exposed of a crowd of faces with flambeaus intermingled fluctuating on the further side of the court. The gateway and the main area of the court were now cleared for the entrance of the cavalry; and the great extent of the court was expressed by the remote distance at which the crowd seemed to stand. Then came the entrance of the dragoons, which was a superb expression of animal power. The ground continued to ascend even through the gateway and into the very court itself; and to the surprise of Bertram who had never until this day seen the magnificent cavalry of the English army, the leading trooper reined up tightly, and spurred his horse, who started off with the bounding ramp of a leopard through the archway. Bertram's horse was the sixtieth in the file; and, as the course of the road between him and the gates lay in*

*a bold curve, he had the pleasure of watching this move-
ment as it spread like a train of gun-powder, or like a
race of sun-beams over a corn-field through the whole
line a-head of him: it neared and neared: in a moment
he himself was carried away and absorbed into the vortex:
the whole train swept like a hurricane through the gloomy
gateway into the spacious court flashing with unsteady
lights, wheeled round with beautiful precision into line,
halted and dressed.*[26]

The enormous scale implied by this description, the
dramatic chiaroscuro and the pride of military pomp are
all familiar traits of De Quincey's imaginative writings.
Here, as elsewhere in this work, one perceives the effort
to raise the common materials of Gothic romance to the
ideal elevation of poetry. In this endeavor, which today
seems so inauspicious, he sometimes comes very close to
success. His failure to achieve more along these lines is
not to be explained by any lack of inspiration, but simply
by the lack of good opportunities. His astonishing re-
sponsiveness to even the slightest and least promising pictorial suggestions has already been noticed in the paper on
Arndt; and here again, in this recast of *Walladmor* one
sees him struggling to transform the wretched material of
his source into a series of splendid tableaux. But being
dependent to such a great extent upon suggestions offered
by casually chosen and frequently unfruitful texts, he often
wasted his talents.

Thomas De Quincey was a great scenic artist, always
waiting for an opportunity to practice his art. But description, except perhaps in poetry, does not constitute an
independent literary form; the descriptive writer must
have always some other purpose. Had De Quincey
possessed even to a slight degree the inventive powers
of a novelist, or had he possessed the knowledge necessary for writing a grand panoramic history such as that

of Gibbon, doubtless he would have been able to provide *himself* with the opportunities he required to achieve
his great effects. Unfortunately, however, he was devoid
alike of the novelist's talent and the historian's knowledge.
Recognizing this deficiency, he sought to remedy it in a
curious way. Toward the end of his life he suggested to his
friend James Hogg that they collaborate upon a gigantic
twelve-volume history of England, Hogg writing the narrative part and De Quincey supplying the illustrative portions.[27] He could have made the same sort of proposal to
a historical novelist, for with De Quincey it was not a
question of fact as opposed to fiction. He exercised his
talents in much the same way in every department of literature. He treated Arndt, the German chronicler, in exactly
the same manner as he treated Alexis, the German novelist.
The only consideration of importance for a writer like De
Quincey was the opportunity afforded by a literary assignment for the sort of descriptive elaboration which was the
essence of his art.

It must not be assumed, however, that De Quincey's
descriptive genius was stimulated only by grandiose events
and romantic themes. There was, as Mario Praz has pointed
out, another and at first sight very incongruous aspect of
his imagination which expressed itself in small, realistic
genre-paintings full of accurate and minutely observed detail.[28] This art, which Praz characterizes by the epithet
Biedermeier, is just as characteristic of De Quincey as is the
grand romantic tableau; and its practice likewise is stimulated by the requirements of his sources.

2

It has already been shown how De Quincey introduced into his *Autobiographic Sketches* several papers
purportedly drawn from personal knowledge, but actually
derived wholly from books.[29] One of these papers, the brief

account of the life and character of Miss Elizabeth Smith, is found among the group of sketches of De Quincey's neighbors at Grasmere entitled "The Society of the Lakes."[30]

All of the other people described in this series—the Lloyds, the Sympson family, John Wilson—were individuals whom De Quincey knew quite well. But of Miss Smith he writes: "[She] had died some months before I came into the country. But yet, as I was subsequently acquainted with her family . . . and as, moreover, with reguard to Miss Elizabeth Smith herself, I came to know more than the world knew—drawing my knowledge from many of her friends, but especially from Mrs. Hannah More, who had been intimately connected with her: for these reasons, I shall rehearse the leading points of her story." (ɪɪ, 404)

The "story" consists of an extremely close summary of the circumstances of Miss Smith's short life. Commencing with an enumeration of the lady's remarkable linguistic and intellectual accomplishments—by the age of twenty-one she had mastered French, German, Spanish, Latin, Greek, and Hebrew, had studied algebra and geometry, and was adept at music and drawing—De Quincey swiftly carries his reader through the course of her life, cramming his pages with exact information about the changing fortunes of her family, her own courageous efforts to sustain her parents amidst hardships, and finally concluding with an extended quotation from an account of Miss Smith's last hours drawn up by her mother.

To a student familiar with De Quincey's practices such a detailed résumé immediately suggests a printed source, probably a biography, from which he could have obtained his abundant information. No hints are to be found in the text, save for some scrappy quotations from letters and the excerpt from the mother's account of her daughter's death; however, in this case, Masson supplies the clue. In a footnote designed to identify the subject of the paper, he alludes to a collection of Miss Smith's literary remains, which proves to be De Quincey's source. The full title of this volume is: *Fragments in Prose and Verse by Miss Elizabeth Smith, lately deceased, with some account of Her Life and Character by H. M. Bowdler* (Bath, 1810).

A check of Bowdler's biographical memoir shows that De Quincey extracted from it the factual information to fill his pages. And in this there is nothing of special interest, for it is that same process of drawing up an abstract from an undisclosed source book, already encountered in many another paper. However, what is of concern here is something quite different—the derivation of the most interesting portion of De Quincey's paper, a weird story which cannot be found in Bowdler, though it was probably suggested by something De Quincey read in the *Fragments*.

Most of the writings contained in the *Fragments and Verses* are formal literary compositions—for example, a translation of the Book of Job, and a life of Klopstock. But in addition, there are a number of feebly written occasional verses, one of them a very curious little poem describing a terrible psychological experience. The editor's notation on the poem reads: "The circumstance which gave occasion to the following reflections, happened exactly as it is here described." And here in their entirety are the verses:

Patterdale, Feb. 1801.

Alone on the pathless steep I wander'd,
I sought the foaming waterfall;
And high o'er the torrent's brink I clamber'd,
Which loud and dreadful roar'd beneath.

At length I came where a winter's streamlet
Had torn the surface from the earth;
Its bed was fill'd with dry shelving gravel,
Which slid beneath my hands and feet.

The pebbles roll'd rattling down the steep slope,
  Then dash'd into the dark abyss,
I follow'd—there was nought to save me,
  Nor bush, nor rock, nor grass, nor moss.

Then did I tranquilly my life resign;
  'If 'tis the will of God that here
'I perish, may that will be done!' but sudden
  Across my mind th' idea flash'd—

' 'Twas not by his command I hither came;
' 'Tis I, who wickedly have thrown away
'That life which He for nobler ends had giv'n.'
Then, with a deep repentence for my fault,
And firm reliance on his mighty pow'r,
I pray'd to him who is, who fills all space,
'Oh Lord, deliver me! I know Thou cans't!'
Instant I rais'd my eyes, I know not why,
And saw my sister stand a few yards off;
She seem'd to watch me, but she could not help.
Then, as the busy brain oft sees in sleep,
I thought she saw me slip into the stream,
And dash rebounding on from rock to rock.
Swiftly she ran all down the mountain side
To meet below my mangled lifeless limbs,
And tatter'd garments.—Life then had value,
It was worth a struggle, to spare her soul
That agony.—I pass'd, I know not how,
The danger; then look'd up—she was not there,
Nor had been! 'Twas perhaps a vision sent
To save me from destruction. Shall I then
Say that God does not heed the fate of mortals,
When not a sparrow falls without his will,
And when He thus saved a worm like me?
So when I totter on the brink of sin,
May the same mercy save me from the gulph![31]

The experience so dimly traced in these halting verses was undoubtedly genuine, but the poem is so vague that the subject seems imaginary. Evidently Miss Smith had been climbing some rocky hills seeking a "foaming water-fall," when she suddenly lost her footing and found herself sliding down into a "dark abyss." The ideas that passed through her mind at this moment undoubtedly succeeded one another with lightning-like rapidity; but in the lumbering verse in which they are presented they seem to have taken far more time than the situation would allow. In any case, her first thought was simply to abandon herself to death; yet this impulse, recorded with such unnatural calm, was immediately checked by the realization that she would be wickedly throwing her life away. Stricken in her conscience, she prayed for deliverance, and then immediately beheld her sister standing nearby. But her sister could not help her; and it was only when she imagined the pain with which her sister would contemplate her mangled body that she suddenly found the strength to struggle for her life. At this moment the apparition of her sister suddenly vanished, and Miss Smith speculated that the figure of her sister was a vision sent to save her from destruction.

In all of this one can perceive a plausible psychological sequence, though the temperament of the woman appears rather abnormal. From the literary point of view the strangest thing about these verses is their abstractness and want of circumstantial substance. This has the effect of making the experience itself seem totally unreal, the product of a very weak imagination.

Now, on the basis of De Quincey's romantic proclivities, as these are revealed in his recast of Arndt's *Recollections,* one would be likely to assume that in treating this incident he would invest it with a wealth of vivid detail, and, at the same time, heighten its suggestions of horror and elaborate upon its morbid psychology. The fact is, though, that he

takes a different tack and, while adding all those circumstances that would make the incident real, changes quite
completely its essential character. Before beginning his
narrative, De Quincey quite simply says that he had the
story "from an account drawn up by Miss Smith herself,
who was most literally exact and faithful to the truth in
all reports of her own personal experiences." (II, 413) Here
is De Quincey's version of Miss Smith's story:

For half an hour or more, she continued to ascend: and,
being a good "cragswoman," from the experience she
had won in Wales as well as in northern England, she
had reached an altitude much beyond what would generally be thought corresponding to the time. The path
had vanished altogether; but she continued to pick out
one for herself amongst the stones, sometimes receding
from the force,[32] sometimes approaching it, according
to the openings allowed by the scattered masses of rock.
Pressing forward in this hurried way, and never looking
back, all at once she found herself in a little stony
chamber, from which there was no egress possible in
advance. She stopped and looked up. There was a frightful silence in the air. She felt a sudden palpitation at her
heart, and a panic from she knew not what. Turning,
however, hastily, she soon wound herself out of this
aerial dungeon; but by steps so rapid and agitated, that,
at length, on looking round, she found herself standing
at the brink of a chasm, frightful to look down. That
way, it was clear enough, all retreat was impossible; but,
on turning round, retreat seemed in every direction alike
even more impossible. Down the chasm, at least, she
might have leaped, though with little or no chance of
escaping with life; but on all other quarters it seemed
to her eye that at no price could she effect an exit, since
the rocks stood round her in a semi-circus, all lofty, all
perpendicular, all glazed with trickling water, or smooth

as polished porphyry. Yet how, then, had she reached the point? The same track, if she could hit that track, would surely secure her escape. Round and round she walked; gazed with almost despairing eyes; her breath became thicker and thicker; for path she could not trace by which it was possible for her to have entered. Finding herself grow more and more confused, and every instant nearer to sinking into some fainting fit or convulsion, she resolved to sit down and turn her thoughts quietly into some less exciting channel. This she did; gradually recovered some self-possession; and then suddenly a thought rose up to her, that she was in the hands of God, and that He would not forsake her. But immediately came a second and reproving thought—that this confidence in God's protection might have been justified had she been ascending the rocks upon any mission of duty; but what right could she have to any providential deliverance, who had been led thither in a spirit of levity and carelessness? I am here giving her view of the case; for, as to myself, I fear greatly that, if her steps were erring ones, it is but seldom indeed that nous autres can pretend to be treading upon right paths. Once again she rose; and, supporting herself upon a little sketching-stool that folded up into a stick, she looked upwards, in the hope that some shepherd might, by chance, be wandering in those aerial regions; but nothing could she see except the tall birches growing at the brink of the highest summits, and the clouds slowly sailing overhead. Suddenly, however, as she swept the whole circuit of her station with her alarmed eye, she saw clearly, about two hundred yards beyond her own position, a lady, in a white muslin morning robe, such as were then universally worn by young ladies until dinnertime. The lady beckoned with a gesture and in a manner that, in a moment, gave her confidence to advance—how she could not guess; but, in some way that baffled

all power to retrace it, she found instantaneously the out-
let which previously had escaped her. She continued to
advance towards the lady, whom now, in the same moment, she found to be standing upon the other side of
the force, and also to be her own sister. How or why
that young lady, whom she had left at home earnestly
occupied with her own studies, should have followed
and overtaken her filled her with perplexity. But this
was no situation for putting questions; for the guiding
sister began to descend, and, by a few simple gestures,
just serving to indicate when Miss Elizabeth was to approach and when to leave the brink of the torrent, she
gradually led her down to a platform of rock, from which
the further descent was safe and conspicuous. There Miss
Smith paused, in order to take breath from her panic, as
well as to exchange greetings and questions with her
sister. But sister there was none. All trace of her had
vanished; and, when, in two hours after, she had reached
her home, Miss Smith found her sister in the same
situation and employment in which she had left her; and
the whole family assured her that she had never stirred
from the house.

(II, 413–15)

If one were not familiar with De Quincey's practice of
rewriting and sometimes reconceiving the incidents and
the descriptions he found in his sources, the first question
one would ask about this little tale is whether it was actually
derived from Elizabeth Smith's curious verses. As he did
not know the lady, and as he actually stated that he was
following her own account of the experience, the derivation
seems likely. A much more interesting question, though, is
why he chose to alter the character of the incident, and,
moreover, why he described it in such a minutely realistic
manner.

Comparing the tale with the poem, one finds that De

Quincey has retained only two elements: the perilous situation of the lady, considerably modified so as to reduce the terror; and the mysterious appearance of the apparition. Although he does attribute to Miss Smith certain reflections suggested by her predicament, the immediate despair and the passionate strain of self-reproach that he found in his source has been entirely suppressed. Likewise, he has rejected the most interesting psychological feature of the experience: the renewal of the lady's will to live produced by the thought of her sister's grief.

The rationale for De Quincey's treatment of this incident is perhaps to be found in the general nature of his account of Miss Elizabeth Smith. He presents her as the model of a young English gentlewoman, as a refined lady of extraordinary accomplishments. The supernatural element in her poem must have attracted his interest; and it would have been like him to have seen in it an opportunity to present an interesting anecdote. However, he was not going to have his idealized lady sprawling on the side of a mountain, perhaps with her clothes in disarray and her mind full of hysterical ideas. And so in order to transform her terrific experience into the sort of predicament appropriate to such a genteel creature, he reduced her hysteria to a mere perturbation of spirits. When the mood was upon him, De Quincey could play the part of the maiden aunt to perfection; and it is really very funny to see to what lengths he carried his notions of female gentility. As for the realistic manner he adopted, perhaps that is best explained as a technique for making the apparition more plausible. If he had told his story in a style anything like that of the original, the apparition would have appeared to be a figment of the lady's over-wrought imagination. But by telling the story in the most matter-of-fact tone and with an abundance of realistic detail, he compels his reader to accept the apparition just as he accepts everything else in the story. Thus instead of the fantasies of a hysterical woman, the reader finds an accurate and authentic ghost story.

It would appear, then, that it is as characteristic of De Quincey to reconceive his subject in realistic terms as to elaborate upon it in the Romantic manner. When the theme is domestic, or when he is dealing with women or children, he invariably adopts the fine manner of a miniaturist; but when representing a dream or a picturesque scene, he aspires to the grand style.

De Quincey's ability to transform even the smallest and humblest circumstance into a vivid and delightful domestic idyll is clearly revealed in his essay on George and Sarah Green, the simple Westmoreland peasants who perished in a snow storm in the mountains of the English Lake District.[33]

De Quincey's source of information was, as he himself relates, a "simple but fervid memoir" drawn up several weeks after the calamity by Dorothy Wordsworth, who was a witness to the frantic efforts to locate the missing pair, and who assumed, with her brother, a portion of the responsibility for the Greens' six orphan children. The memoir was not available to De Quincey at the time he wrote his paper; and therefore some of his deviations from Miss Wordsworth's account are probably due to lapses of memory.[34] However, the substantial differences between De Quincey's paper and his source are not to be explained as accidents of recollection, but as the result of an entirely different intention.

The memoir that Dorothy composed at the instance of her brother had an immediate practical purpose; it was to to be an instrument in the appeal for funds made at the time on behalf of the orphan children. And in examining Dorothy's *A Narrative Concerning George and Sarah Green of the Parish of Grasmere addressed to a Friend*,[35] one perceives in the very proportions of the account the purpose for which it was designed. The memoir comprises forty-seven pages: the fate of the Greens occupies only five pages; another nine are taken up with the search for the bodies, the funeral, and the other events Dorothy observed; seventeen pages are devoted to the disposition of the children in various homes in the neighborhood; the concluding fourteen pages present Dorothy's impression of the Greens —their lives, their characters, and the nature of the family group.

De Quincey's paper, which is a narrative of the death of the Greens, is for the most part based on only the first five pages of Dorothy's memoir. Yet since his paper is almost as long as hers, he has obviously introduced much original matter. He begins with a long and lingering description, beautifully drawn, of the remote vale of Easedale—ringed by mountains and shut off from the neighboring hamlets. It was here that the Greens lived; but as their death occurred on the other side of the mountains, facing Grasmere, this description would appear to be little more than a beautiful adornment.

After this quiet prelude, De Quincey introduces the Greens on their way to a country auction. The auction is pleasantly described, and at its conclusion the reader watches the old people going off on their fatal trip across the mountains. At this point De Quincey interrupts the narrative and shifts his attention to the six children who had been left alone at home and are now anxiously awaiting their parents' return. It is the eldest child, Agnes, a little girl of eight, who especially excites one's admiration as she bustles about superintending the smaller children and making preparations for the night. De Quincey's description of her actions is extremely minute.

> *having caused all her brothers and sisters—except the two little things, not yet of a fit age—to kneel down and say the prayers which they had been taught, this admirable little maiden turned herself to every household task that could*

have proved useful to them in a long captivity. First of all, upon some recollection that the clock was nearly going down, she wound it up. Next, she took all the milk which remained from what her mother had provided for the children's consumption during her absence and for the breakfast of the following morning,—this luckily was still in sufficient plenty for two days' consumption (skimmed or "blue" milk being only one half penny a quart, and the quart a most redundant one, in Grasmere),—this she took and scalded, so as to save it from turning sour. That done, she next examined the meal chest; made the common oatmeal porridge of the country . . . ; but put all of the children, except the two youngest, on short allowance; and, by way of reconciling them in some measure to this stinted meal, she found out a little hoard of flour, part of which she baked for them upon the hearth into little cakes; and this unusual delicacy persuaded them to think that they had been celebrating a feast.

(XIII, 136–37)

According to De Quincey's account, the children remain snowbound for three full days until finally, the weather letting up, the eldest girl—now suffering intense anxiety, but firmly maintaining her composure—manages to make her way to a neighboring farm where her news is received with horror and from where the alarm is immediately spread over the district.[36]

The representation of the children and their self-sustaining activities occupies almost one-half of De Quincey's narrative of the events. And when at last he returns to the fate of George and Sarah Green, the warmth and excitement that pervaded his treatment of the children visibly fades, and the narrative ends rather lamely.

Now, from even this brief summary it will be evident that De Quincey's interest in this story was not centered on what is nominally its subject—the death of George and Sarah Green. Rather, his imagination was excited by the condition of the children and their struggles to sustain themselves. It is interesting from this point of view to discover how few suggestions he derived from the details of Dorothy Wordsworth's report. Of the child Agnes, whose name was really Jane, and whose age was eleven, not eight, Dorothy Wordsworth reports only that:

> She had nursed the Baby, and, without confusion or trouble, provided for the other Children who could run about: all were kept quiet—even the Infant that was robbed of its Mother's breast. She had conducted other matters with perfect regularity, had milked the cow at night and morning, wound up the clock, and taken care that the fire should not go out.[37]

Here again, one has an example of De Quincey's imagination kindling at some slight suggestion contained in his source; and again one encounters the technique of the genre painter—in this instance meticulously detailing a little picture of domestic activity. The two best portions of this paper—the evocation of the vale of Easedale and the genre study of the children—are both descriptions, and both are clearly related to the theme of isolation and abandonment that must have been stirring in De Quincey's mind as he drew up his account.

3

The sources for the "Revolt of the Tartars"[38] have already been the subject of elaborate investigations, including an entire doctoral dissertation. But the effect of all these studies has been to perplex what is in fact a relatively simple question.

The paper itself contains no acknowledgment of authorities save for one footnote reading: "All the circumstances of the Chinese Emperor's actions are learned from a long state paper upon the subject of this Kalmuck migration drawn up in the Chinese language by the Emperor himself. Parts of this paper have been translated by the Jesuit missionaries. The Emperor states the whole motives of his conduct and the chief incidents at great length." (vii, 411 n) David Masson took this reference at face value, and in his independent edition of the *Revolt* he argued that De Quincey had made use of a paper entitled "*Monument de la Transmigration des Torgouths des Bords de la Mer Caspienne dans l'Empire de la Chine,*" which is found in the great collection of *Mémoires concernant les Chinois*, published in 1776 by the Jesuit missionaries to Pekin.[39] But there was an obvious difficulty in this initial ascription. The Jesuit memoir, a little paper of twenty-seven pages, contains only the final episodes of the history that De Quincey relates, and it in fact presents a much different interpretation of the events.

Years later, when Masson was preparing his collected edition of De Quincey's writings, he turned up a fresh clue in a footnote to "Homer and the Homeridae." The note reads: "Some years ago I published a paper on the Flight of the Kalmuck Tartars from Russia. Bergmann, the German from whom that account was chiefly drawn, resided for a long time among the Kalmucks, etc." (vi, 88) With this explicit reference Masson easily identified the source as Benjamin Bergmann's *Nomadische Streifereien unter den Kalmüken in den Jahren 1802 und 1803* (*Nomadic Wanderings with the Kalmucks in the Years 1802 and 1803*).[40] Bergmann's book consists of a number of letters describing his life among the Tartars, interspersed with independent dissertations on the history and culture of the Kalmucks. Masson discovered that De Quincey had drawn upon a paper of 106 pages entitled "*Versuch zur Geschichte der Kalmükenflucht von der Wolga.*"[41] Masson also found a French translation of Bergmann, published in the year 1825, under the title *Voyage de Benjamin Bergmann chez les Kalmuks.*[42]

It was from this French translation of Bergmann that De Quincey had quoted the Jesuit memoir. It is, therefore, surprising that Masson did not relinquish his earlier hypothesis that De Quincey had used the original Jesuit memoir. One finds him summing the matter up thus in an introductory note to volume VII of his edition: "I have no doubt left that it was Bergmann's Essay of 1804 that supplied De Quincey with the facts, names, and hints he needed for filling up that outline-sketch of the history of the great Tartar Transmigration of 1771 which was already accessible for him in the Narrative of the Chinese Emperor Kien Long, and in other Chinese State Papers, as these had been published in translation in 1776 by the French Jesuit missionaries." (VII, 9)

Masson's hypothesis that the "Revolt of the Tartars" was based on several different sources has been further elaborated in a doctoral dissertation by Joseph A. Sandhaas.[43] His extensive collection of translated "Source Material," assembled with the intention of testing the historical accuracy of De Quincey's account, really obscures the question completely by presenting as De Quincey's sources those primary documents upon which Bergmann drew. Moreover, Sandhaas translates Bergmann's dissertation from the German as De Quincey's primary source, although the evidence indicates that it was actually the French translation that De Quincey used. Erhart H. Essig, in his doctoral dissertation, follows Sandhaas in assuming that the German text was De Quincey's source.[44]

A careful examination of the whole matter, however, strongly suggests that, as usual, De Quincey had only one source, the most recent and most accesssible publication on the subject. The French translation of Bergmann was published in 1825; and in a letter to William Blackwood, dated March 3, 1830, De Quincey first proposes the subject of the Tartar flight.[45] Not only does De Quincey quote directly from the French translation;[46] but his spelling of all the proper nouns follows the French form and not the German.[47] As the French translation is exact, the difference between it and the German original is really immaterial; but there is no reason to believe that De Quincey worked from the German text, and there is certainly no evidence that he was familiar with documents as inaccessible as those Sandhaas presents.

Bergmann's treatise concerns the emigration of a Tartar tribe in the eighteenth century from their homeland on the Russian border of the Russian empire to the western fringes of China, two thousand miles distant. Bergmann takes up the subject by stating that though the emigration as an historical occurrence is sufficiently well known, having been the subject of several studies and numerous literary and historical allusions,[48] the causes of the event have never been properly elucidated, nor has its course been accurately delineated. His treatment, then, is divided into two portions: the first, a long and discursive analysis of the conditions that produced the revolt; the second, a short and sketchy résumé of such incidents of the flight as had been reported by trustworthy authorities. Apparently most of his information was derived from Russian sources and pertained either to the conditions that existed in the Tartar horde prior to the commencement of the revolt or to the early stages of the flight, when the Tartars were still within the periphery of the Russian empire. He did not have the information to follow the Tartars deep into the remote regions of central Asia, and so at this point in his résumé even the suggestion of narrative is lost. It is not until the Tartars enter Chinese territory that he is able to pick up the thread by reporting the facts of their reception contained in the paper composed by the Jesuit missionaries to Pekin. To this very inadequate summary he appends a special report of the experiences of Captain Weseloff, a Russian trade commissioner who had been stationed among the Tartars and had been carried off by them as a hostage. Bergmann's essay, then, is not so much a narrative of a sequence of remarkable events as it is a causal analysis of a perplexing historical phenomenon.

Although written with an avowed purpose of criticism and scholarly analysis, Bergmann's account of the Tartar revolt and flight is curiously romantic. It assumes that this colossal event was produced primarily by the political intrigues of a single man—Zebek-Dorchi, the Tartar prince, who had some claim to the title of Khan, or ruler of the Tartar horde. Dorchi belonged to the same family as the ruling Khan, Oubacha, but his rights had been ignored by the Russians when Oubacha's father had been presented with the title in an unlawful alteration of the succession. Dorchi's aims were revenge upon the Russians and the recovery of his title, both of which he sought to achieve by political machinations. His opponent in the struggle for power was the weak but amiable Khan. In his description of the two men it is obvious that Bergmann conceives of Zebek-Dorchi as a villain and Oubacha as his victim.

> Such were Oubacha and Zebek-Dorchi. Once one understands these two characters thoroughly, it is not difficult to foresee the direction which the affairs of the Kalmucks were likely to take. Here frankness and loyalty, there finesse and astuteness; here ideas far removed from all suspicion of evil, there intrigues that overwhelm the soul; in the former a confidence too facile and a lack of resolution, in the latter a deceptive appearance of justice and an extraordinary perseverance in the pursuit of a plan to its final accomplishment: his plan once conceived, it is clear that the former would fall into the nets of the latter.[49]

Bergmann established the two principal characters of the story, the noble but naïve Oubacha and the relentless and designing Zebek-Dorchi. Although he accuses Zebek-Dorchi of fomenting the revolt, he does acknowledge that without the concurrence of favorable circumstances the conspiracy would never have succeeded. There was, for example, a certain prophecy that influenced the Tartars to leave Russia that year; there were other powerful men in the horde who hoped to gain through Zebek-Dorchi's plots; and there was the fact that the Tartars had come from China not long before.

De Quincey found in the conspiracy reported by Bergmann a theme of melodramatic interest. It was a case of a single individual, intent on power, destroying the lives and happiness of tens of thousands of his countrymen. And so one finds in the first portion of De Quincey's paper—which, like its source, leads up to the actual events of the flight—a skillful presentation of the conspiracy. All those adventitious circumstances that combined to produce the revolt, however, are now presented as calculated steps in a grand scheme of revenge. De Quincey writes in the manner of the ratiocinative analyst: if Zebek-Dorchi had intended revenge upon the Russians, and if he had once preferred a claim to the throne, then his scheme of revenge would encompass both these goals. A revolt and flight of the Tartar horde would dismay the Russians and create conditions favorable for his own assumption of power. If there was to be a flight, there must perforce be a destination, and this must be one that would ensure the Tartars against retribution. The Chinese empire, being both distant and powerful, would serve the purpose perfectly. But if such a scheme was to be carried out, Zebek-Dorchi must needs have accomplices, and these he must choose for their power and loyalty to himself. To persuade the people, a prophecy must be forthcoming; and so on through the entire sequence of events up to the time of the revolt. De Quincey thus strengthens Bergmann's notion of a conspiracy by drawing it out step by step with the rigor of a logician. However, with the groundwork so thoroughly laid, the conspiracy must be ultimately resolved in terms of its final intention. For this purpose De Quincey found nothing in his source he could use and so he resolved the conspiracy by inventing two episodes. In one of these Zebek-Dorchi sends his assassins to murder the Khan; and in the other he is himself murdered, according to the strictest poetic justice, by the Chinese Emperor.

De Quincey's treatment of the conspiracy of Zebek-Dorchi is ingenious and effective; but it serves merely as an introduction to what was clearly intended as the principal matter of interest—the actual narrative of the Tartar flight. In treating this subject, he makes no real effort to follow the dim and irregular outline afforded by Bergmann's résumé of the events. Instead he employs Bergmann merely as a reservoir from which to draw outlandish names, bits of descriptive detail, and suggestions for battles, intrigues, and calamities. The plan of the narrative was evidently conceived as a whole, and De Quincey has relied largely upon his own imagination to fill in the details.

The central fact of the emigration was simply the movement of a vast number of people across the vague and immense regions of Central Asia. To render this monstrous scene, De Quincey divides his imaginary map into a series of geographical sections, limited by an arbitrary arrangement of natural features—rivers, plains and mountains—some of them purely fictitious. Within each of the panels of this panoramic mural, he draws, in graphic detail, some striking event or situation, such as a battle, a siege, or a scene of suffering and desolation. And to implement this design further he adds suitable backgrounds of geographic and climatic features—descriptions of wastelands, blizzards and scorching heats. Before the final debacle he introduces a highly romantic episode based upon Bergmann's account of the adventures of Weseloff; and when this little *divertissement* has been played out, he abruptly presents the final scenes, terminating in the savage meleé at Lake Tengis.

This comprehensive arrangement is wholly De Quincey's, as are practically all the incidents and details that it comprises. Nevertheless, one does discern a consistent use of the scanty materials provided by the source, these being

freely altered and rearranged in accordance with his conception or theme. There are, in fact, three interrelated
themes which, in his introduction, De Quincey makes explicit, lest they be missed by the hasty magazine reader.

> *Few cases, perhaps, in romance or history, can sustain a
> close collation with this as to the complexity of its sep-
> arate interests. . . . 1st, That of a conspiracy, with as close
> a unity in the incidents, and as much of a personal in-
> terest in the moving characters, with fine dramatic con-
> trasts, as belongs to "Venice Preserved," or to the "Fi-
> esco" of Schiller. 2dly, That of a great military expedi-
> dition, offering the same romantic features of vast dis-
> tances to be traversed, vast reverses to be sustained, un-
> tried routes, enemies obscurely ascertained, and hard-
> ships too vaguely prefigured, which mark the Egyptian
> expedition of Cambyses—which mark the anabasis of the
> younger Cyrus, and the subsequent retreat of the ten
> thousand—which mark the Parthian expeditions of the
> Romans, especially those of Crassus and Julian—or (as
> more disastrous than any of them, and, in point of space
> as well as in amount of forces, more extensive) the Rus-
> sian anabasis and katabasis of Napoleon. 3dly, That of
> a religious Exodus, authorized by an oracle venerated
> throughout many nations of Asia,—an Exodus, there-
> fore, in so far resembling the great Scriptural Exodus of
> the Israelites, under Moses and Joshua, as well as in the
> very peculiar distinction of carrying along with them
> their entire families, women, children, slaves, their herd
> of cattle and of sheep, their horses and their camels.*
>
> (VII, 369–70)

The first theme, the conspiracy against the state, has already been discussed. The flight which De Quincey viewed
under the double aspect of a military expedition and a
national exodus will now be considered.

Conceiving the flight partly in terms of a military expedition, De Quincey was obliged to invent some appropriate battles, for in his source he found only faint suggestions of what must have been mere skirmishes. And so with the help of the knowledge gained through years of reading military histories, he has imagined two complementary engagements. First, he stages a "bloody and exterminating battle" in which an entire tribe is decimated by the pursuing Cossacks. Then, with an eye to poetic justice, he reverses the fortunes of his imaginary wars and allows the Kalmucks to win in a lively engagement at a disputed mountain pass. In both of these battles he is indebted to his source for little more than the barbaric names of the defeated clan, Feka-Zechorr, and the mountain pass, Ouchim.

The glamor of a military campaign was not De Quincey's primary interest in relating the flight of the Kalmuck Tartars. It was, rather, to his third theme, his association of the flight with the Biblical Exodus, that he looked for his most telling effects. To invoke Biblical associations he found it necessary, however, to alter Bergmann's description of the character of the Tartars. Unlike the children of Israel, they were a savage people, and the atrocities they committed upon their Russian captives are clearly described in Bergmann's account. This characterization would never do for De Quincey's purpose, as he intended to portray the sufferings of a simple, pastoral people victimized by wicked rulers. Thus all the references to atrocities are suppressed, and the sufferings and calamities of the long march are developed with every appropriate circumstance.

As the time of year at which the flight began was winter, De Quincey graphically describes the suffering of the people, compelled to travel through blizzards and bitter cold. However, according to Bergmann the spring came very early that year, and it was not the cold but softness of the ground that troubled the Tartars on their march.[50] At one point, evidently seeking to provide some contrast to the sense of incessant movement which the narrative suggests, De Quincey sketches a delightful idyll, in which the people camp for ten days amidst the newly fallen snow and recreate themselves with feasting and merriment. But soon they are driven off by the pursuing Russian army, which relentlessly pursues them with its "terrible artillery." Actually, as one learns from Bergmann, the Russian pursuit was sluggish and half-hearted and was soon given over.

To magnify the impressiveness of the exodus, De Quincey increases the number of Tartars from Bergmann's figure, seventy-five thousand, to an astonishing six hundred thousand. Likewise, he enormously increases the distances, so that if one were to add up all his references, one should perhaps discover something like six or eight thousand miles between the Volga and China.

One of De Quincey's greatest problems was avoiding the sense of monotony generated by the sameness of the Tartar sufferings. To provide a contrast, just before the grand catastrophe of his piece he introduces a romanticized version of the adventures of Weseloff, the Russian captive. Bergmann reports only that Weseloff, after having been carried a great distance by the Tartars, finally found a means to escape from his captors and to return to Russia. In De Quincey's version the Captain becomes the center of an episode in which Zebek-Dorchi lures the Khan into a death trap. At the moment when the Khan is desperately fighting for his life, surrounded by assassins, Weseloff suddenly appears and saves him. The Khan expresses his gratitude in the polished phrases of a European courtier and sends the Captain off with his blessings.

After this artificial interlude, De Quincey returns to the main course of the narrative; and here he achieves one of his most effective contrasts. After briefly reviving the reader's impressions of the exhausted Tartars—now thousands of miles from their point of departure and reduced to a third of their original number—he abruptly changes the point of view and presents a charming and refreshing picture of the Chinese Emperor, Kien Long, taking his pleasure at a hunting lodge improbably situated near the margin of the Gobi Desert. The Emperor in his pavilion and his Chinese "yagers" with their silver trumpets have all the delicacy of porcelain figures. And it is through their calm eyes that one witnesses the final debacle at Lake Tengis.

At first the oncoming Tartars are glimpsed indistinctly through voluminous masses of desert sand and vapor.

> suddenly to the westwards there arose a vast cloudy vapour, which by degrees expanded, mounted, and seemed to be slowly diffusing itself over the whole face of the heavens. By and by this vast sheet of mist began to thicken towards the horizon, and to roll forward in billowy volumes. . . . Through the next hour, during which the gentle morning breeze had a little freshened, the dusty vapour had developed itself far and wide into the appearance of huge aerial draperies, hanging in mighty volumes from the sky to the earth; and at particular points, where the eddies of the breeze acted upon the pendulous skirts of these aerial curtains, rents were perceived, sometimes taking the form of regular arches, portals, and windows, through which began dimly to gleam the heads of camels "indorsed" with human beings—and at intervals the moving of men and horses in tumultuous array—and then through other openings or vistas at far distant points the flashing of polished arms. But sometimes, as the wind slackened or died away, all those openings, of whatever form, in the cloudy pall would slowly close, and for a time the whole pageant was shut up from view; although the growing din, the clamours, shrieks, and groans, ascending from infuriated myriads, reported, in a language not to be misunderstood, what was going on behind the cloudy screen.

(VII, 411–12)

For this passage there is no suggestion in Bergmann; however, it is anticipated in several of De Quincey's early writings where one finds his favorite metaphor of columns of sand which, drawn up by the desert winds, assume a variety of impressive forms and then mysteriously dissolve and vanish.[51] After sighting the Tartars from the Emperor's pavilion, De Quincey has the reader ascend the mountains overlooking Lake Tengis and cast his eyes down upon the horrors enacting below. This extraordinary vision, the most celebrated piece of bravura description to be found in all of De Quincey's writings, was suggested by the following notice in Bergmann:

> These fugitives . . . , without even taking off their clothes, hurled themselves into a herd with their beasts and sank into the midst of the waters as far as the depth of the lake allowed, in order to appease the thirst which devoured them so cruelly. Many were victims of their own imprudence; an even greater number succumbed to the weapons of the Kirghises in a new and bloody battle. Lacking the means to defend themselves, the most nimble of the Kalmucks hardly had time to cross the river and thus to escape their enemies.[52]

De Quincey's version of the scene is unforgettable.

> Upon this last morning, at the sight of the hills and the forest scenery, which announced to those who acted as guides the neighbourhood of the lake of Tengis, all the people rushed along with maddening eagerness to the anticipated solace. The day grew hotter and hotter, the people more and more exhausted, and gradually, in the general rush forwards to the lake, all discipline and command were lost—all attempts to preserve a rearguard were neglected—the wild Bashkirs rode in amongst the encumbered people, and slaughtered them by wholesale, and almost without resistance. Screams and tumultuous shouts proclaimed the progress of the massacre; but none heeded—none halted; all alike, pauper or noble, continued

to rush on with maniacal haste to the waters—all with faces blackened by the heat preying upon the liver, and with tongue drooping from the mouth. The cruel Bashkir was affected by the same misery, and manifested the same symptoms of his misery as the wretched Kalmuck; the murderer was oftentimes in the same frantic misery as his murdered victim—many indeed (an ordinary effect of thirst) in both nations had become lunatic, and in this state, whilst mere multitude and condensation of bodies alone opposed any check to the destroying scimitar and the trampling hoof, the lake was reached; and into that the whole vast body of enemies together rushed, and together continued to rush, forgetful of all things at that moment but of one almighty instinct. This absorption of the thoughts in one maddening appetite lasted for a single half-hour; but in the next arose the final scene of parting vengeance. Far and wide the waters of the solitary lake were instantly dyed red with blood and gore: here rode a party of savage Bashkirs, hewing off heads as fast as the swathes fall before the mower's scythe; there stood unarmed Kalmucks in a death-grapple with their detested foes, both up to the middle in water, and oftentimes both sinking together below the surface, from weakness or from struggles, and perishing in each other's arms. Did the Bashkirs at any point collect into a cluster for the sake of giving impetus to the assault? Thither were the camels driven in fiercely by those who rode them, generally women or boys; and even these quiet creatures were forced into a share in this carnival of murder, by trampling down as many as they could strike prostrate with the lash of their fore-legs. Every moment the water grew more polluted; and yet every moment fresh myriads came up to the lake and rushed in, not able to resist their frantic thirst, and swallowing large draughts of water, visibly contaminated with the blood of their slaughtered compatriots. Wheresoever the lake was shallow enough to allow of men raising their heads above the water, there, for scores of acres, were to be seen all forms of ghastly fear, of agonising struggle, of spasm, of death, and the fear of death—revenge, and the lunacy of revenge—until the neutral spectators, of whom there were not a few, now descending the eastern side of the lake, at length averted their eyes in horror.[53]

(VII, 414–16)

4

Unlike so many of his papers that first were published, according to the practice of the time, without their author's name, De Quincey's "Spanish Military Nun"[54] on its first appearance in the numbers of *Tait's Edinburgh Magazine* for May, June and July, 1847, bore prominently beneath the original title, "The Nautico-Military Nun of Spain," the byline "By Thomas De Quincey." This is ironic in view of the fact that in this paper alone among all his numerous recasts and *rifacimenti* may De Quincey be taxed with something very close to plagiarism.

In his introduction to the original publication De Quincey presents his material with his accustomed show of learned authority. Anticipating doubts about the accuracy and authenticity of this bizarre narrative, he writes:

No memoir exists, or personal biography, that is so trebly authenticated by proofs and attestations, direct and collateral. From the archives of the Royal Marine at Seville, from the autobiography of the heroine, from contemporary chroniclers, and from several official sources scattered in and out of Spain, some of them ecclesiastical, the amplest proofs have been drawn and may yet be greatly extended, of the extraordinary events here recorded.

(XIII, 247)

With such a prelude, one cannot help but be rather puzzled by the ambiguous tone of what follows:

Monsieur de Ferrer, a Spaniard of much research, and originally incredulous as to the facts, published about seventeen years ago a selection from the leading documents, accompanied by his palinode as to their accuracy. His materials have been since used for the basis of more than one narrative, not inaccurate, in French, German and Spanish journals of high authority. It is seldom that French writers err by prolixity. They have done so in this case. The present narrative, which contains no one sentence derived from any foreign one, has the great advantage of close compression; my own pages, after equating the size being as 1 to 3 of the shortest continental form.
(XIII, 248)

After this authoritative enumeration of the original materials, with its implications of comprehensive knowledge, one finds it odd that De Quincey should conclude by commending his own paper for such slight advantages as originality of diction and greater conciseness as compared with other treatments of the same subject. In fact, one suspects an equivocation, for surely had he been familiar with the original materials, De Quincey would not have measured his own presentation by merely expository standards.

One comes a little closer to the truth in a postscript that De Quincey appended to the reprint of the article in his collected edition of 1854. Here he frankly disclaims immediate knowledge of the primary materials. "I must not leave the impression upon my readers that this complex body of documentary evidences has been searched and appraised by myself. Frankly, I acknowledge that, on the sole occasion when any opportunity offered itself for such a labour, I shrank from it as too fatiguing." (XIII, 241–42) Even in the postscript, though, the closest he comes to divulging his real source is this discreet allusion contained in his notice of the previous writings on the subject. "[The history has been] reported at length by journals of the highest credit in Spain and Germany, and by a Parisian journal so cautious and so distinguished for its ability as the *Revue des Deux Mondes.*" (xiii, 241)

David Masson, catching at the hint afforded by De Quincey's allusion to the *Revue des Deux Mondes*, traced the source of this paper to an article in that magazine entitled "Catalina de Erauso," which appeared in the issue of the fifteenth of February, 1847, just two and a half months before the publication of the first installment of De Quincey's composition.[55]

The original French article, which runs to a length of forty-nine large pages, is a very ably written narrative based upon M. de Ferrer's edition of a seventeenth-century manuscript life, *Vida y sucesos de la Monja alferez dona Catalina de Araujo, doncella natural de Saint-Sebastien, escrita por ella* (*Life and Adventures of the Nun Lieutenant Dona Catalina de Araujo, Native Daughter of Saint-Sebastian, Written by Herself*). The author of the French article, Alexis de Valon, characterizes the manuscript life in these words: "It is less a narrative than the matter for a narrative; it is a dry and terse summary without animation or life."[56] One may therefore safely conclude that in working up the material into his own vivid and finished narrative, Valon employed all his literary skill so as to realize every possibility for description, characterization, and plot sequence implicit in the original. It was, therefore, a skillfully written narrative that De Quincey determined to recast according to his own conception of the subject. And in this fact—that for once he chose to work from a finished literary source—lay one of the difficulties that so seriously impaired the success of his endeavor.

The interest of Valon's treatment of the subject consists entirely in the adventures of the nun, which are extraordinary in themselves and which are presented with considerable graphic effect and with a firm grasp on the narrative sequence. As De Quincey has transferred to his article the entire series of adventures, neither adding nor omitting a single episode, it is perhaps pertinent to summarize the related actions of the French article.

At the commencement of the narrative the heroine, Catalina, though she has spent all of her fifteen years in a convent, is described as having neither the appearance nor the manner of a young woman. Haughty and insolent in temperament, and masculine in manner, she desires nothing more than to escape from the restraints of conventual life. At the first opportunity she slips out of the convent, dresses herself as a man, and sets off for Vitoria where her uncle resides. This kindly old gentleman receives her as a wandering scholar and puts her to Latin grammar. Rather quickly tiring of study, she runs off a second time and makes her way to Valladolid where, after becoming involved in a street brawl, she is picked up by a good-natured courtier who makes her an usher in his house. She is soon forced to relinquish this pleasant existence, however, when her father unexpectedly appears seeking her. This time, determined to make pursuit impossible, she enlists on a ship bound for the Americas.

Off the coast of Peru the vessel is wrecked and Catalina, the sole survivor, finds herself upon a desolate shore. With the good fortune that always accompanies her, she finds her way to the town of Paita where she becomes a clerk to a merchant. Soon she is involved in a desperate scrape, the first in a long career of violence. After killing a man who has insulted her, she is offered the choice of being executed for her crime or marrying a relative of the dead man—a rich and beautiful lady who is in fact the merchant's mistress. The merchant and the lady smuggle Catalina out of prison; but before the marriage can take place, she manages to escape from the city in an open boat. Picked up at sea, she is taken to Concepción where she joins a unit of the Spanish army commanded by her brother. Catalina soon distinguishes herself in battle and is raised to the rank of *alferez*.

She easily acquires the truculent character and bellicose manner of a hardened campaigner. Once, after a session at play, she kills a man who had become enraged by his losses; and on another occasion, acting as second to an officer engaged in a duel at night, she kills her own brother while fighting blindly in the dark.

Stricken with remorse, she deserts the army and crosses the Cordilleras with two renegades who die along the way. This adventure is almost fatal; but her luck still holds and she is rescued by the retainers of a wealthy lady who lives near Tucuman. Again the impossible situation of an offer of marriage arises, this time with the lady's beautiful young daughter, to whom Catalina is strangely attracted. Acceding for the moment to this proposal, she again murders a man who has cheated her at cards, relentlessly tracking him home and running him through on his very doorstep. Again she is arrested and imprisoned. She is brought to trial and found guilty, though only on the evidence of suborned witnesses. Through the exertions of the lady she is reprieved at the foot of the gallows and packed off to Cuzco. On her way to that city, she falls in with a party of travelers—an *alcalda*, his beautiful wife, and another man who is conducting an intrigue with the woman. One night the jealous husband waylays the lover and kills him, the lady fleeing to Catalina for protection. After a wild ride through the night with the husband hot in pursuit, Catalina reaches the city of Cuzco, deposits the lady in a convent, and faces about to receive her pursuers. In the ensuing melee, she accounts for her fifth victim, the *alcalda*; but being herself wounded in the breast—desperately, she fears —she decides to give up the game, confess her true identity, and throw herself upon the mercy of the Church. Having preserved her virginity, she receives absolution and, eventually, a pardon from the Pope. Returning to Spain, she is hailed and feted as a heroine. Years later, sailing to America

on another expedition, she disappears mysteriously never to
be heard from again.

In Valon's straightforward narrative of Catalina's adventures the character of the heroine is left to be inferred from
the nature of her actions; and the judgment the reader
forms of her accords fully with the views of the author expressed in his postscript.

> Her faults, however grave they may be, do not inspire
> disgust. Hers is a savage, self-abandoned nature with a
> conscience for neither good nor evil. Reared to the age
> of fifteen by ignorant nuns, abandoned since this time to
> all the chances of a wandering life, to all the instincts of a
> common nature, Catalina could not have learned any
> other morality than that of the highway, the camp, and
> the fo'c's'le. Evidently, she does know what she is doing.[57]

Now, it was precisely this question of Catalina's true
character that probably inspired De Quincey to attempt a
rifacimento of Valon's entire narrative. He saw Catalina,
not as a primitive creature without a moral sense, but rather
as an innocent and heroic being struggling desperately to
preserve herself and to maintain her honor in a world
of evil men and degrading circumstances. Of course, she
was violent and stained with blood; yet she had never fought
except in defense of her rights. In fact, she "was noble in
many things. Her worst errors never took a shape of self-
interest or deceit. She was brave, she was generous, she was
forgiving, she bore no malice, she was full of truth—qualities that God loves either in man or woman. She hated
sycophants and dissemblers." (XIII, 199–200) And so it
followed for De Quincey that she deserved to be celebrated
by one who could appreciate her real greatness and who
would not, like this Monsieur Valon, treat her as a mere
savage. It is interesting to observe in this connection that
the "Spanish Military Nun" was written in the same year
as the famous rhapsody on Joan of Arc; and while De Quincey had the good sense not to impose upon the rough

figure of Kate the exalted conception of womanhood, of armed and inspired innocence, which he found embodied in Joan of Arc, there can be no doubt about the tendency of his characterization.

To be sure, it was a bold idea, but it was not an impossible one. Such women, it will be recalled, are found in the Jacobean drama, the drama of Catalina's own age. There is Middleton's Moll Cutpurse for one, a character whom T. S. Eliot has enthusiastically described as the type of "a free and noble womanhood." But Middleton was a great poet; and as Aristotle has said, "the poet must be more the poet of his stories or plots than of his verses."[58] Now De Quincey was certainly not the poet of his plots: he was, in fact, the poet of his verses; or rather, he was a master of that element which Aristotle pronounced "the least artistic of all the parts"—the Spectacle. How was a great scenic artist going to solve a problem such as this, which involved the adjustment of an action to the requirements of a character conceived almost independently of the action?

Actually, there was no solution possible in these terms: De Quincey's great descriptive powers could not be profitably invoked on this occasion. His solution was to follow the action exactly as it had been reported in his source, but to change the tone and manner of the relation so that it would read like a picturesque romance of the eighteenth century. The grim realism of Valon's rendition he would expunge with humor; the ugly actions of the heroine he would present as violent bouts of farce; and her sufferings and heroic achievements he would heighten romantically.

De Quincey's strategy was not well chosen in view of his powers and limitations; but he was struggling with intractable material that forced him out of his usual path. The product of this unnatural effort is a very ambivalent sort of treatment—half essay and half narrative, half grotesque farce and half lyric rhapsody. In endeavoring to reconcile the harsh facts of Valon's account with his own idealized conception of Catalina, De Quincey was compelled to present the story obliquely, interposing between the reader and the events his own personality as a sophisticated and humorous raconteur. Unfortunately, his humor often degenerates into facetiousness: he reduces the seriousness of his heroine's actions without really altering their character.

De Quincey's difficulties were increased, one suspects, by the fact that his source was so firmly set in another mold. In general, it may be observed that for a writer like De Quincey, who is dependent for his matter on a source, but who intends to produce something of original value, the best material is that which is suggestive yet unrealized. With a finished literary treatment of the subject before him, De Quincey was constrained; he could not summon up the power necessary to decompose the source into its constituent elements and recast it completely according to his own intention. As has been pointed out earlier, it was just at those points where the source materials were most imperfect, most open and vague, that his imagination produced its most extraordinary effects. Here he found everything finished and closed, with hardly a single opportunity remaining for the interposition of a new idea. However, in one long passage—definitely the most impressive section of the entire paper—De Quincey does find the opening that one feels him restlessly groping for throughout his long and tortuous progression. It is significant, too, that this flight occurs immediately after a passage in which he has been following Valon very closely, adopting for once the same tone and point of view as that of the original.

In Valon's narrative Catalina is ascending the Cordilleras in the company of two famished and disheartened deserters. She sees a man sitting on top of a hill with a gun in his hand, looking like a hunter on the watch. It is the first human being they have seen for days and their hopes are raised as they imagine some habitation nearby. Valon relates:

The travellers had arrived at a place where enormous blocks of stone reared themselves like dark waves in the middle of the snow. The heroine sought in vain, in the shelter of these stones, some of those bushes that had enabled them sometimes to light a small fire; all vegetation had disappeared; at these heights, man alone has a right to live. Then, not knowing what to do nor what step to take, she decided, in order to better orient herself, to climb on one of the blocks of stone from where her view would embrace a more extensive horizon. She raised herself painfully, attained the most elevated summit of these small mountains and looked around her. Suddenly she uttered a cry and ran again toward her companions. Seated and supported against a neighboring rock, a man had appeared to her! What could this traveller be? He was a liberator perhaps, and without doubt he was not alone! The announcement of unexpected help gave courage to the two dying ones; they got up and followed Catalina. Having arrived twenty feet from the designated place, they perceived the stranger, who had not moved from his place. He was seated, half hidden behind a corner of rock, in the position of a sharpshooter on the look-out or of a hunter on the watch. "Who's there?" cried Catalina, raising her arquebuse with effort. The stranger did not answer, did not move and did not appear to have heard. "Who's there?" repeated Catalina. This second summoning was as vain as the first. The three travellers advanced slowly, with caution, along the side of the rock, and arrived finally two feet from the silent look-out whose back was turned to them. "Eh! friend," said Catalina striking him on the shoulder, "are you sleeping?" But hardly had she pronounced these words, than she recoiled three paces, becoming pale with terror. At the touch of Catalina, the seated man had rolled on the snow like an inert mass. It was a frozen corpse, stiff as a statue; his face was blue and his mouth half-open in a frightful smile.[59]

Here is De Quincey's free translation:

They had reached a billowy scene of rocky masses, large and small, looking shockingly black on their perpendicular sides as they rose out of the vast snowy expanse. Upon the highest of these that was accessible Kate mounted to look around her, and she saw—oh, rapture at such an hour!—a man sitting on a shelf of rock, with a gun by his side. Joyously she shouted to her comrades, and ran down to communicate the good news. Here was a sportsman, watching, perhaps, for an eagle; and now they would have relief. One man's cheek kindled with the hectic of sudden joy, and he rose eagerly to march. The other was fast sinking under the fatal sleep that frost sends before herself as her merciful minister of death; but, hearing in his dream the tidings of relief, and assisted by his friends, he also staggeringly arose. It could not be three minutes' walk, Kate thought, to the station of the sportsman. That thought supported them all. Under Kate's guidance, who had taken a sailor's glance at the bearings, they soon un-threaded the labyrinth of rocks so far as to bring the man within view. He had not left his resting-place; their steps on the soundless snow, naturally, he could not hear; and, as their road brought them upon him from the rear, still less could he see them. Kate hailed him; but so keenly was he absorbed in some speculation, or in the object of his watching, that he took no notice of them, not even moving his head. Coming close behind him, Kate touched his shoulder, and said, "My friend, are you sleeping?" Yes, he was sleeping—sleeping the sleep from which there is no awaking; and, the slight touch of Kate having disturbed the equilibrium of the corpse, down it rolled on the snow: the frozen body rang like a hollow iron cylinder; the face uppermost, and blue with mould, mouth open, teeth ghastly and bleaching in the frost, and a frightful grin upon the lips.

(XIII, 193–94)

The imaginative excitement produced by rendering this ghastly scene evidently released the impeded powers of De Quincey's mind, and in the pages which immediately

follow he breaks free for a space from the constraints of
his source and imagines the terrible ordeal of Kate's descent
alone from the Cordilleras. His source is here quite per-
functory.

> Towards evening, she thought she saw a tree in the
> distance; she was returning therefore toward the country
> of the living! She gathered all that remained in her of
> strength and energy, and walked so well, that she
> finally reached this tree of safety; but there her courage
> betrayed her; her trembling limbs gave way; she extended
> herself on the ground and fell into a state which was at
> one and the same time a faint and a sleep. This torpor
> lasted all night; when she came to herself, day was
> dawning, the temperature was relatively very mild and
> the tepid air smothered her.[60]

The thought of his heroine's sufferings carried De Quincey's imagination through one of those characteristically
hallucinatory episodes with which one is familiar from
the dream sequences in the *Confessions*. The passage is
celebrated for its extraordinary sense of delirious movement.

> *Oh! verdure of human fields, cottages of men and
> women (that now suddenly, in the eyes of Kate, seemed
> all brothers and sisters), cottages with children around
> them at play, that are so far below—oh! spring and sum-
> mer, blossoms and flowers, to which, as to his symbols,
> God has given the gorgeous privilege of rehearsing for
> ever upon earth his most mysterious perfection—Life,
> and the resurrections of Life—is it indeed true that poor
> Kate must never see you more? Mutteringly she put that
> question to herself. . . . Dimmed and confused had been
> the accuracy of her sensations for hours; but all at once
> a strong conviction came over her that more and more
> was the sense of descent becoming steady and continu-
> ous. Turning round to measure backwards with her eye
> the ground traversed through the last half-hour, she
> identified, by a remarkable point of rock, the spot near*

which the three corpses were lying. The silence seemed deeper than ever. Neither was there any phantom memorial of life for the eye or for the ear, nor wing of bird, nor echo, nor green leaf, nor creeping thing that moved or stirred, upon the soundless waste. Oh, what a relief to this burden of silence would be a human groan! Here seemed a motive for still darker despair. And yet, at that very moment, a pulse of joy began to thaw the ice at her heart. It struck her, as she reviewed the ground from that point where the corpses lay, that undoubtedly it had been for some time slowly descending. Her senses were much dulled by suffering; but this thought it was, suggested by a sudden apprehension of a continued descending movement, which had caused her to turn around. . . . Frightful was the spasm of joy which whispered that the worst was over. It was as when the shadow of midnight, that murderers had relied on, is passing away from your beleaguered shelter, and dawn will soon be manifest. It was as when a flood, that all day long has raved against the walls of your house, ceases (you suddenly think) to rise. . . . Kate faced round in agitation to her proper direction. She saw, what previously, in her stunning confusion, she had not seen, that hardly two stonethrows in advance lay a mass of rock, split as into a gateway. Through that opening it now became certain that the road was lying. Hurrying forward, she passed within these natural gates. Gates of paradise they were. Ah, what a vista did that gateway expose before her dazzled eye! what a revelation of heavenly promise! Full two miles long, stretched a long narrow glen, everywhere descending, and in many parts rapidly. All was now placed beyond a doubt. She was descending,—for hours, perhaps, had been descending insensibly,—the mighty staircase. Yes, Kate is leaving behind her the kingdom of frost and the victories of death. . . . And very soon, as the crest of her new-born happiness, she distinguished at the other end of that rocky vista a pavilion-shaped mass of dark green foliage —a belt of trees, such as we see in the lovely parks of England, but islanded by a screen of thick bushy undergrowth! Oh! verdure of dark olive foliage, offered suddenly to fainting eyes, as if by some winged patriarchal herald of wrath relenting—solitary Arab's tent, rising with saintly signals of peace in the dreadful desert— must Kate indeed die even yet, whilst she sees but cannot reach you! Outpost on the frontier of man's dominions, standing within life, but looking out upon everlasting death, wilt thou hold up the anguish of thy mocking invitation only to betray? Never, perhaps, in this world was the line so exquisitely grazed that parts salvation and ruin. As the dove to her dovecot from the swooping hawk—as the Christian pinnace to the shelter of Christian batteries from the bloody Mahometan corsair—so flew, so tried to fly, towards the anchoring thickets, that, alas! could not weigh their anchors, and make sail to meet her, the poor exhausted Kate from the vengeance of pursuing frost.

And she reached them; staggering, fainting, reeling, she entered beneath the canopy of umbrageous trees. But, as oftentimes the Hebrew fugitive to a city of refuge, flying for his life before the avenger of blood, was pressed so hotly that, on entering the archway of what seemed to him the heavenly city gate, as he kneeled in deep thankfulness to kiss its holy merciful shadow, he could not rise again, but sank instantly with infant weakness into sleep—sometimes to wake no more; so sank, so collapsed upon the ground, without power to choose her couch, and with little prospect of ever rising again to her feet, the martial nun.

(XIII, 201–4)

In this sequence, the lyrical and the pictorial aspects of De Quincey's imagination are fused into a flowing panorama in which every detail has the preternatural vividness of a dream. It is description in movement, the movement of the body and of the eye descending over falling ground and glimpsing with hectic joy the promise of life. This moment of impassioned prose is all that De Quincey could achieve in the long and dreary effort of recounting with strained and awkward humor the adventures of the nun-lieutenant.[61] As a whole, the paper fails to achieve the effect for which it was intended. Ultimately, Kate is never—at any moment but in the passage over the Andes— the being towards whom De Quincey's fantasies streamed.

5

De Quincey's failure to recast completely Valon's narrative of the adventures of Catalina de Erauso to bring the story into line with his clear and passionately held view of the heroine is a significant indication of his limitations as a creative artist. In the elaboration of descriptions, in the lyric expression of emotion and in the evocation of dreams and reveries, De Quincey was without a peer; however, in all that relates to character, action, and plot his was decidedly a minor talent. In narrative he was essentially the raconteur. He could relate an anecdote so skillfully that what was originally a mere trifle became an interesting and exciting tale. He could take an incident or situation and weave about it so rich an investiture of diction and descriptive detail that it became an impressive and unforgettable scene. But he did not possess the inventive and adaptive capacities of a real fabulist. Unlike the novelist, he could not create a world of living people engaged in significant actions.

There is one composition, however, which might seem to be an exception to the general rule, and that is the "Postscript" to "On Murder Considered as One of the Fine Arts."[62] This terrifying tale of murder, with its background of lower-class life in London and its elaborately contrived suspense, reminds one more of the work of Dickens, Dostoevsky, and Poe than it does of the generality of De Quincey's writings. The "Postscript" is unique among De Quincey's works because for once he essayed a theme suggested, not by exotic books or high-flown fantasies, but by the sordid record of human experience provided by the daily press. His source in this case was the original newspaper reports of the notorious Williams murders committed in London in the year 1811. Most critics who have discussed the "Postscript" have assumed that a source so inadequate and formless as a newspaper account could not have significantly determined the character of a composition distinguished preeminently for imagination and art. And when one learns that the newspaper reports which suggested this story appeared more than forty years before its composition, it seems almost certain that De Quincey must have worked independently or with only the slightest support from his source. However, as shall be seen, in this case as in so many others, De Quincey's source, by the opportunities it provided and by the limitations it imposed, determined the design of his narrative and his conception of the theme.

The "Postscript" was written at the very end of De Quincey's life—during the period in which he was wholly engaged in the task of revising and arranging his writings for the collected edition. This enormous labor occupied him from the year 1853 until his death in 1859. The "Postscript," which appeared in 1854 in the fourth volume of the collected edition, was the only new work of any significance (apart from the extensive additions to the *Confessions*) produced in this six-year period. From the feverish and superfluent style of the piece, it would appear that, like so many of De Quincey's finest writings, this paper was written in great haste, perhaps while the printer's devil stood at the door. Since in the last years of his life

De Quincey found original composition unbearably pain-
ful, one cannot but suppose that an extraordinarily powerful impulse drove him to the labor of writing this long
and complicated story.[63] At least, he must have realized
that it was his last opportunity to tell the tale that had
obsessed him for over forty years.

For the Williams murders in 1811 had from the first
occupied a prominent position in De Quincey's mind. By
the time of the essay "On the Knocking at the Gate in
Macbeth" (1823)—an essay inspired by one incident of
these crimes—he had formulated his peculiar view of
Williams as the greatest of all practitioners of the "art" of
murder. In the introduction to this essay he describes
Williams as having "made his *début* on the stage of Ratcliffe Highway, and executed those unparalleled murders
which have procured for him such a brilliant and undying
reputation." (x, 390) The esthetic view of murder suggested by this remark was developed at great length four
years later in the extravagant "On Murder Considered as
One of the Fine Arts (First Essay)," which is a treatment
of murder modelled along the lines of Aristotle's analysis
of tragedy in the *Poetics*. Just as Aristotle holds up Sopho-
cles as the greatest of the tragic poets, the one whose works
approximate most closely to the ideal, so De Quincey in
his humorous way exalts John Williams as the perpetrator
of those murders "the sublimest and most entire in their
excellence that ever were committed." (xiii, 43) But De
Quincey makes no effort to describe these masterpieces,
because "nothing less than an entire lecture, or even an
entire course of lectures, would suffice to expound their
merits." (xiii, 43) Recent research has established the
curious fact that, shortly after the publication of this
essay, De Quincey did attempt some narratives of famous
murders; but they were not the Williams murders, and
they were so badly written that William Blackwood refused to publish them.[64] In 1839 De Quincey published

a second essay on murder as a fine art, and again he alludes to Williams' "great exterminating *chef-d'oeuvre.*" (XIII, 58) It was, therefore, a fully matured, though long inhibited, conception that finally broke through the ring of conscious restraints and inspired De Quincey to a furious burst of creative activity.

The first problem that arises in studying this paper in relation to its source is the exact determination of what De Quincey read. When the murders were first reported in the London newspapers, De Quincey was not in the city but three hundred miles away at Grasmere. It is very probable, however, that he read one of the metropolitan newspapers, since it is known that during the period of the Peninsular Wars he and Wordsworth anxiously followed the course of events as they were reported in the London press. Sometimes they would walk for miles at night to meet the carrier coming up from Ambleside with the latest dispatches. Of course, one cannot know which paper De Quincey read; but, as it turns out, this is a matter of indifference, because many of the London newspapers reproduced, more or less exactly, the reports published in the *Times.*[65]

The first thing that strikes one in digging out the old newspapers and comparing them with De Quincey's narrative is the extraordinary accuracy with which he has presented the crimes. Were there not so many other examples of his remarkable powers of memory, one would be forced to assume that at some time not long before the composition of his narrative he had looked over an old file of newspapers to revive his faded impressions. This, though, would be contrary to his usual procedure, and in fact there are enough mistakes in minor details—names, dates, and the like—to make it probable that he was working from memory.[66]

As for the murders, according to the London papers, they were committed on midnight of December 7, 1811,

and not, as De Quincey has it, 1812. John Marr, who kept
a lace and pelisse warehouse at 29 Ratcliffe Highway in
London, was killed along with his wife, his shopboy, and
four-month-old infant by some unknown assailant who
was evidently intent on robbery. The victims were hide-
ously butchered and, as one would expect, the crime caused
a sensation. The account in the *Times* of December 9 is
headed "Horrid Murders," and the story underneath begins: "We almost doubt whether, in the annals of murders,
there is an instance on record to equal in atrocity those
which the following particulars will disclose." The initial
report is long and circumstantial, and for days afterwards
the newspaper is full of the details of the coroner's inquest,
the activities of the Bow Street Police, and the various
offers of rewards totalling five hundred pounds. Gradually,
though, as all the suspects are released and the clues exhausted, the spate of news diminishes. Then, suddenly, on
the night of December 19, again at midnight and in the
same neighborhood of Ratcliffe Highway, another family
was massacred. This time the victims were an elderly man
named Williamson, the keeper of the King's Arms public
house, his wife, and an old serving woman. Their little
granddaughter, who was asleep upstairs, was spared because
a lodger made good his escape from the second story of the
house and roused the watch, thus forcing the criminal to
flee through a back window.

On December 23, a sailor named John Williams was
interrogated by the magistrates and held as a suspect. After
several days of intense questioning, during which he stead-
fastly defended himself, Williams committed suicide in
his cell. The investigation was pursued for some days
after the death of Williams until enough circumstantial
evidence was accumulated to place his guilt beyond doubt.

Such is the outline of the Williams murders as best one
can make out from the stories in the London newspapers.
And such, too, is the outline of De Quincey's famous tale.

He has taken over the entire sequence of events, neither adding nor omitting a single incident. As for the details necessary for filling in this sketch—the facts concerning the murderer's appearance, character and motivation, the way in which the crimes were committed, the locale of Ratcliffe Highway, and the character and lives of the victims—all this information is very inadequately supplied by the newspapers. The motive of the murderer, for example, is far from clear. At first it appears to be robbery; but then one discovers that all Williams' victims were friends or former friends; that he had once been Marr's shipmate; and that he frequented Williamson's public house until the night of the murder. Williams himself is a rather enigmatic figure. He is described as a typical sailor, ordinary in appearance, neat in dress, popular with women, and given to drinking and brawling. There is nothing in the newspaper description of Williams that would mark him as the perpetrator of such monstrous crimes.

The newspapers, of course, are quite exact where names, dates, and circumstances are concerned. One learns from them the occupations of the victims and a few details of their lives, the exact locations of the houses, and some facts about the neighborhood in which the murders were committed. As there were no witnesses to the crimes, all that anyone can discover about the murders themselves is what can be inferred from the position of the corpses.

However, on the occasion of each crime, there was a single individual who, though not a witness to the murders, did accidentally come upon the scene immediately afterwards and while the murderer was still at work. The Marr's serving woman, Margaret Jewell, had been sent out to purchase some oysters for the family's supper shortly before the time when they were all murdered. And this girl, in her deposition at the coroner's inquest, recounted in great detail her efforts to get into the house when she returned. She had banged on the door and rung the bell. She had thought she heard a footstep within the house. She had become alarmed and had spoken to the watch. Her noise had finally awakened a neighbor who went around behind the house and, entering by the back door, had discovered the bodies weltering in gore. In the case of the Williamson murders there was a lodger named John Turner who deposed that, having been awakened by a noise below stairs, he had heard cries of "murder." Arising from bed naked, he had descended the stairs—not realizing what he was doing—and had actually caught a glimpse of a man in a bearskin coat stooping over the body of Mrs. Williamson and rifling her pockets. Horrified by the sight, he had crept upstairs to his own room, thrown up the window, tied the sheets of his bed together, and descended to the ground, falling into the arms of the watch.

De Quincey's intention was to create from these various materials a full-blown tale of murder and horror, organized around his central perception of the crimes as deliberately achieved masterpieces of the art of murder. He begins with the artist himself, John Williams.

The murderer of the "Postscript" is De Quincey's most awesome character, a weird and dandified villain, cold-blooded and calculating—a fiend. The common Irish sailor of the newspaper reports has been completely transformed. The fresh complexion heightened by wind and weather has turned sallow and sick, a greenish yellow. The sandy hair has become a lurid shade, something between yellow and red, dyed in imitation of certain Indian cults. The neat sailor's clothing has been discarded and the evil one appears attired in a long surtout lined with silk, handsomely turned out like a dandy. The face, hardly mentioned in the newspapers, was an inviting blank that De Quincey fleshed out with glazed eyes, mean features, and a horrid expression. One might expect that De Quincey would motivate his villain just as ingeniously as he has described him. But no, he simply repeats the rumors and speculations found in his source. Actually, the motive was not essential to his conception of the crime, for in studying the story further, the reader soon perceives that Williams is not really a character at all. After glimpsing him briefly at the beginning of the narrative, one never sees him again, except for a moment—and at that, obliquely— through the terrified eyes of Mr. Williamson's lodger. The murderer Williams is a *presence* in De Quincey's story; one senses him at his appalling work through every page and every moment of the relation. But he is only an idea, a reflex in the reader's mind of the horrible deeds he commits.

Williams' victims, though, those very ordinary people— Marr, the young tradesman, and Williamson, the old publican—are treated in a much different manner. Here De Quincey had an opportunity to produce some of those little realistic genre pictures, those slightly sentimental representations of everyday life that are recognizable as his imaginative response to themes of a private and domestic nature. The description of the Marr household is particularly good, with the struggling young tradesman working late on a Saturday night in his shop, while down in the back kitchen his sweet young wife tends her infant child in its cradle. The handsome shopboy and the loyal serving girl round out the picture of the family of a typical London tradesman.

Once the victims have been described bustling about in their house, quite oblivious to the danger which threatens from the sinister figure who stands in the shadows across the street eyeing the shopfront, one is ready to see the crimes enacted and the victims falling before the murderer's onslaught. But De Quincey intends something very different; and though he has keyed his readers up to the anticipation of murder, just at the critical moment he withdraws his attention from the scene of the crime and takes off on a long divagation following the movements of the servant girl who had been sent out to buy the family's supper. This movement might appear to be an artifice for increasing the suspense; but in fact it was not so much an artifice as a necessity. De Quincey had not, as has been noted, any adequate account of the murders themselves. His problem, then, was to achieve the full effect of horror appropriate to these crimes without representing the crimes themselves. His source did supply him with a full account of the doings of a person who had come within the field of the murderer's activity. By making the experiences of Margaret Jewell the objective correlative of that emotion of mounting horror, the intended grand effect, De Quincey triumphantly surmounted the limitations imposed upon him by his source. The scene in which Margaret—or Mary, as De Quincey calls her— listens at the door of the Marr house to the footfall of the murderer within is one of the most thrilling moments in Romantic literature. It was a scene that Dostoevsky admired and imitated in *Crime and Punishment*.[67] To quote it out of context necessarily diminishes the effect; yet, it is still fascinating to see what De Quincey made of his source in this one instance. First, though, here is an extract from Margaret Jewell's deposition.

I was out about 20 minutes and when I returned, I found my master's shop and door closely shut, and there was no sign of light: I rang the bell, but received no answer. While I continued ringing repeatedly at the door, the watchman passed by with a person in charge: about this time I certainly heard a foot on the stairs, and I thought it was my master coming to let me in; I also heard the child cry in a low tone of voice; I rang then again and again, and knocked at the door with my foot; while I was doing so a man came up to me, abused me very much, and used very insulting language to me: I thought I'd wait until the watchman should come: he came at last, called one o'clock, and desired me to move on; I told him I belonged to the house, and that I was locked out.[68]

And now for De Quincey's realization of this moment.

She had not in the first moment of reaching home noticed anything decisively alarming. . . . Mary rang, and at the same time very gently knocked. She had no fear of disturbing her master or mistress; them she made sure of finding still up. Her anxiety was for the baby, who, being disturbed, might again rob her mistress of a night's rest. And she well knew that, with three people all anxiously awaiting her return, and by this time, perhaps, seriously uneasy at her delay, the least audible whisper from herself would in a moment bring one of them to the door. Yet how is this? To her astonishment, —but with the astonishment came creeping over her an icy horror,—no stir nor murmur was heard ascending from the kitchen. At this moment came back upon her, with shuddering anguish, the indistinct image of the stranger in the loose dark coat whom she had seen stealing along under the shadowy lamp-light, and too certainly watching her master's motions: keenly she now reproached herself that, under whatever stress of hurry, she had not acquainted Mr. Marr with the suspicious appearances. . . . But all such reflections this way or that were swallowed up at this point in overmastering panic. That her double summons could have been unnoticed— this solitary fact in one moment made a revelation of horror. One person might have fallen asleep, but two— but three—that was a mere impossibility. And, even supposing all three together with the baby locked in sleep, still how unaccountable was this utter—utter silence! Most naturally at this moment something like hysterical horror overshadowed the poor girl, and now at last she rang the bell with the violence that belongs

to sickening terror. This done, she paused: self-command
enough she still retained, though fast and fast it was
slipping away from her, to bethink herself that, if any
overwhelming accident had compelled both Marr and
his apprentice-boy to leave the house in order to summon
surgical aid from opposite quarters—a thing barely sup-
posable—still, even in that case Mrs. Marr and her infant would be left, and some murmuring reply, under
any extremity, would be elicited from the poor mother.
To pause, therefore, to impose stern silence upon herself, so as to leave room for the possible answer to this
final appeal, became a duty of spasmodic effort. Listen,
therefore, poor trembling heart; listen, and for twenty sec-
onds be still as death! Still as death she was; and during
that dreadful stillness, when she hushed her breath that
she might listen, occurred an incident of killing fear, that
to her dying day would never cease to renew its echoes
in her ear. She, Mary, the poor trembling girl, checking
and overruling herself by a final effort, that she might
leave full opening for her dear young mistress's answer
to her own last frantic appeal, heard at last and most
distinctly a sound within the house. Yes, now beyond
a doubt there is coming an answer to her summons.
What was it? On the stairs,—not the stairs that led
downwards to the kitchen, but the stairs that led upwards to the single storey of bedchambers above,—was
heard a creaking sound. Next was heard most distinctly
a footfall: one, two, three, four, five stairs were slowly
and distinctly descended. Then the dreadful footsteps
were heard advancing along the little narrow passage to
the door. The steps—oh heavens! whose steps?—have
paused at the door. The very breathing can be heard of
that dreadful being who has silenced all breathing except
his own in the house. There is but a door between him
and Mary. What is he doing on the other side of the
door? A cautious step, a stealthy step it was that came

down the stairs, then paced along the little narrow passage—narrow as a coffin—till at last the step pauses at the door. How hard the fellow breathes! He, the solitary murderer, is on one side the door; Mary is on the other side. Now, suppose that he should suddenly open the door, and that incautiously in the dark Mary should rush in, and find herself in the arms of the murderer. Thus far the case is a possible one—that to a certainty, had this little trick been tried immediately upon Mary's return, it would have succeeded; had the door been opened suddenly upon her first tingle-tingle, headlong she would have tumbled in, and perished. But now Mary is upon her guard. The unknown murderer and she have both their lips upon the door, listening, breathing hard; but luckily they are on different sides of the door; and upon the least indication of unlocking or unlatching she would have recoiled into the asylum of general darkness.

(xiii, 86–89)

The scene at the door is the climax of De Quincey's narrative. He does, finally, present his reconstruction of the murders, but only in the style of a ratiocinative analyst, inferring what must have happened from the evidence of the corpses. Here as elsewhere in his narrative, he has reproduced all the available materials with astonishing accuracy.

The second set of murders is treated exactly like the first, the great moment again being a scene worked up from the deposition of a person who had brushed the murderer and survived. To the narrative of the Williams murders De Quincey added a report of the McKean murders, committed in the year 1826, at a small village near Manchester called Winton. His source was again a newspaper report; but this time one of the survivors witnessed the actual murder and described it graphically in his deposition. As one might expect, in this narrative De Quincey represents directly the horrible scene: a serving woman, whose throat has been cut from ear to ear and who has been left for dead by the murderer, slowly rises from the floor and turns about to walk down the stairs like a bloodstained ghost.

After this long investigation one perceives that in his treatment of the Williams and McKean murders, De Quincey has proceeded just as he has done on many another occasion: ingeniously developing the materials provided him by his source so as to realize to the utmost possible extent all the latent possibilities for picturesque description and emotional effect. A close reading of the "Postscript" will show that it is not essentially a narrative of actions involving characters who have motives, passions and personalities; rather it is a rhapsody of horror swelling to three great crescendos, in which the theme of impending disaster is expressed with overwhelming power. Williams, the murderer, is not a character or even a "figure"; he is the invisible and terrible presence of death. The Marrs and the Williamsons are bright little images in a genre-painting; and even Mary, the one person with whom De Quincey could identify himself, becomes simply the vehicle for an emotion that soon engulfs and obliterates her nature. It is not so much narrative that one finds in this paper as it is the minute and exhaustive representation of situations, of isolated incidents distended to the proportions of nightmare.

De Quincey has transformed the prosaic record of sordid crime into an idealized vision of horror; but he has achieved the effect of art by enforcing the character of truth. And from this point of view one gains a fresh insight into his oft-repeated statement that the Williams murders were the products of a great artist. What he means, of course, is that for once life itself had wrought like an artist, and adventitious circumstances had fallen together into the pattern of tragedy. But the artist was not Williams, the homicidal maniac. It was De Quincey who, with his esthetic perception of reality, envisioned the events like the outline of a drama which he had only to fill in to achieve the effect of deliberate art.

Miner or Minter?

THIS INVESTIGATION of De Quincey's use of printed source materials was undertaken with a very limited object in view; it was not anticipated that the original study would have to be extended to practically all of De Quincey's work. As the research proceeded, however, it gradually became clear that what had originally appeared to be occasional borrowings were, in fact, merely the most obvious instances of De Quincey's consistent practice of appropriating literary materials and working them up into magazine articles. Having examined in the course of this study twenty-eight compositions written in all periods of De Quincey's career—ranging from novels to short articles and including several examples of his best work—the author is convinced that De Quincey's dependence on printed sources is the key to his literary career.

For not only does the study of De Quincey's sources explain the extreme multifariousness of his writings and his relative success or failure in many instances, but also it provides the solution to the much-discussed problem of his curiously inconsistent style. The present study does raise a number of questions that have yet to be considered. For one thing, it will be asked whether there is any likelihood that there are other works derived from sources which this investigation has failed to uncover. No certain answer can be given to this question, but it is likely that most of the borrowings in the scholarly papers have now been

ascertained. The most promising subjects for future inquiry
are De Quincey's two principal works of fiction, his Gothic
novel *Klosterheim* and his *novella, The Avenger.*

Klosterheim[1] was written in 1831 in response to a grave
financial crisis which was worsened by William Blackwood's refusal to make De Quincey any further advances
on future articles.[2] Like most magazine journalists who do
not supplement their income by editorial work, De Quincey
was generally unable to live on the income from his
writings and was frequently forced to ask for money on
the strength of his past performances and future utility
to the magazine. It should be noted that he was paid very
little for his work, receiving no more from Blackwood than
the going rate—ten guineas the sheet, that is, ten guineas
for each sixteen pages of the magazine.[3] He had toyed
for many years with the idea of writing a novel, a kind of
work for which he had little aptitude, but which would,
if he were successful, bring him a substantial sum. He had
long had a contract with Blackwood, who had agreed to
pay him one hundred pounds for a three hundred-page
novel. When Blackwood refused him any further advances,
De Quincey wrote to ask if his old contract still held; and
evidently receiving a favorable reply, he set to work on the
book, which he completed in time for publication early in
1832.[4] As always, he lavished great pains on the writing,
and the style of *Klosterheim* was warmly praised by so
discriminating a critic as Coleridge.[5] The book caused no
stir, to be sure, but it was certainly not a performance of
which the author need have been ashamed. There was
something about it, however, that troubled him; for in
later years, when James T. Fields requested the right to
publish the novel in the American edition of De Quincey's
works, permission was refused.[6] Nor did De Quincey include it in the English collected edition. Since several of
De Quincey's plagiarized pieces were included in his collected edition, the fact that he was unwilling to have this

work reprinted is not of itself a very significant indication of indebtedness. Nevertheless, it is odd.

In any case, *Klosterheim* exhibits many striking similarities with a certain kind of German fiction popular in this period. The novel, which is set in a town in Swabia during the Thirty Years' War, centers upon the conflict between a villainous Landgrave, who has murdered the former ruler, and the legitimate heir, Maximilian, an officer in the Imperial Army. Moving about the city in disguise, Maximilian tries to subvert the ruling power by freeing prisoners and kidnapping prominent citizens. The Landgrave, in turn, with the help of his subtle adviser, Adorni, plots to identify and destroy the "masque." After a series of melodramatic encounters and escapes, the story culminates in a spectacular scene at a masked ball during which Maximilian appears at the head of the Imperial Army and takes possession of the town.

Klosterheim is closely related to the *Ritter-Räuber-und Schauerromane* that were produced in fantastic abundance during the last years of the eighteenth century and the first third of the nineteenth century in Germany. More particularly, it is in the genre established by Zschokke's *Aballino, der grosse Bandit* (1793), a novel which had wide currency in England through the translation of Matthew Gregory ("Monk") Lewis. In this story a bandit, who is really a nobleman and who employs many disguises, strikes down the enemies of Venice and thus saves the state.

De Quincey's novel employs all the stock incidents and characters found in German works of this genre; and it is possible, of course, that *Klosterheim* is original to the extent of being a pastiche of these conventional elements. From what is known of De Quincey's methods of working, however, it is perhaps more likely that the book is a *rifacimento* of some obscure German original, and the leading American authority on these German novels, Miss

Agnes Genevieve Murphy,[7] concurs with this view. In a letter the author of the present study received from her in 1960, she remarks: "Certainly De Quincey used all the stock incidents and I am inclined to agree with you that he probably plagiarized a German source." The difficulty of locating a source for this novel may be gauged from the fact that the principal collection of German novels of this sort in America, the Lincke Loan Library, which is held by the library of the University of Chicago, contains about eighteen thousand volumes.

The Avenger[8] belongs to the same genre as *Klosterheim*, but it is a shorter work, and not so elaborately written. If one were able to discover the source, he would probably find that it is much more like a translation than a thoroughgoing recast. There is, though, this fact to be considered: when James T. Fields wrote to De Quincey asking him if he were actually the author of *The Avenger*, De Quincey replied affirmatively: "He [De Quincey] sends his kind regards to you [Mrs. Fields] and Mr. Fields, and says that he did write *The Avenger*. It was written under circumstances forcing him to finish it very hurriedly."[9]

In addition to those writings for which one may suppose De Quincey to have had a source—which for obvious reasons he was not willing to reveal—there is another group of papers, wholly legitimate in character, the sources for which are plain from his own statements. Preeminent among these are his publications on the subject of political economy, which occupy one entire volume of the standard edition. These pieces have been carefully studied by specialists, all of whom concur in regarding them as popular expositions of the doctrines of David Ricardo. De Quincey's treatment of Ricardo is typical of the work for which he was naturally suited, and from which, in the more important case of Kant, he backed away. In Ricardo, as in Kant, he discovered a great mind absolutely dominating an important area of thought by means of a highly original and systematically developed philosophy, but suffering in his relation to the educated public from a want of comprehensibility that was not so much the effect of his ideas as of the poor style in which they were set forth. In the first of his papers, "Dialogues of Three Templars,"[10] De Quincey makes a remark that might well serve as the motto for all his expository writings. "For the fact is, that the *labourers of the Mine* (as I am accustomed to call them), or those who dig up the metal of truth, are seldom fitted to be also *labourers of the Mint, i.e.* to work up the metal for current use." (IX, 50–51)

J. R. McCulloch, in his *The Literature of Political Economy* (London, 1845), describes De Quincey's dialogues admiringly: "These dialogues . . . are unequalled, perhaps, for brevity, pungency, and force. They not only bring the Ricardian theory of value into strong relief, but triumphantly repel, or rather annihilate, the objections urged against it by Malthus, in the pamphlet now referred to and in his *Political Economy*, and by Say, and others. They may be said to have exhausted the subject."[11] De Quincey's principal exposition of Ricardo is contained in an independent volume entitled *The Logic of Political Economy* (London, 1844),[12] which is an enlarged version of a series of articles that appeared in *Blackwood's Magazine* under the title "Ricardo Made Easy."[13] This book has been described by Gertrud Meyer in *Das Verhältnis Thomas De Quincey's zur Nationalökonomie* (Freiburg, 1926): "De Quincey endeavors to provide in the form of a practical commentary an introduction into the abstractions of Ricardo. His own contribution consists in additional examples, improvements of logic, mathematical illustrations, and in the effort towards clarity and sharper expression of antitheses."[14]

In addition to these writings on political economy, one must also include in the account of De Quincey's derivative compositions his political writings. W. E. A. Axon lists seventeen articles on political subjects in his enumera-

tion of previously unidentified pieces by De Quincey in
Blackwood's Magazine,[15] and there are several more in the
Masson edition. Not all this material has been carefully
examined for this study, but it quickly becomes apparent
that it is hastily written hack work—as Professor Eaton has
called it, "a slight amount of casual newspaper information wrapped round with settled theory and subtle reflection."[16] A rather less respectful description is given by
Edgar Allan Poe in his humorous essay "How to Write a
Blackwood Article."

> And, after all, it's not so very difficult a matter to com-
> pose an article of the genuine *Blackwood* stamp, if one
> only goes properly about it. Of course I don't speak of
> the political articles. Everybody knows how *they* are
> managed, since Dr. Moneypenny explained it. Mr. Black-
> wood has a pair of tailor's-shears, and three apprentices
> who stand by him for orders. One hands him the *Times*,
> another the *Examiner* and a third a "Gulley's New Com-
> pendium of Slang-Whang." Mr. B. merely cuts out and
> intersperses. It is soon done—nothing but *Examiner*,
> "Slang-Whang," and *Times*—then *Times*, "Slang-Whang,"
> and *Examiner*—and then *Times*, *Examiner*, and "Slang-
> Whang."[17]

In addition, included among De Quincey's derivative
compositions are a number of reviews that are merely sum-
maries of the content of the book under review, and an
extended commentary on the first six books of Plato's *Republic*, much of it a précis of the dialogue.[18] Moreover, in
his original critical writings De Quincey is frequently dependent on contemporary thinkers for ideas and principles;
his debts in this department have been fully demonstrated
by Professor René Wellek.[19]

Setting aside his numerous translations, most of which
are clearly avowed, one finds that De Quincey is dependent
to a greater or lesser degree on literary source materials in
something like sixty per cent of his writings, which, in the
standard edition, comprise fourteen closely printed vol-

umes, averaging 450 pages to the volume. So extensive are his borrowings that the question becomes finally not so much what has De Quincey derived, but rather, where is he really original. And as might be expected, the only compositions that are wholly original are those works of a personal nature in which he has drawn on his own experience—his dreams, his fantasies, his adventures, and his impressions of his friends and acquaintances. Also among his original works are a number of lengthy papers on questions of style, language, and rhetoric.

Instead then of regarding De Quincey, by turns, as a scholar, an historian, an authority on economics, or a novelist, one would do better to treat him for the most part as a very able literary journalist, the sort of writer who takes each assignment as it comes and treats it as best he can with the materials at his disposal. Considered in this light, De Quincey would become the foremost practitioner of that kind of journalism which is designed to enlighten and to entertain the public with themes of an intellectual character. In fact, one can go further and say that the uniqueness of De Quincey's contribution to the journalism of his day consisted just in his conscious and deliberate exploitation of the character and pursuits of the scholar.

When De Quincey embarked on his career in the second decade of the nineteenth century, the now-famous literary magazines were still new enterprises just beginning to establish themselves as an important part of the popular culture of England. The best of the early magazines, *The London Magazine* and *Blackwood's Edinburgh Magazine*, were still experimenting with the public taste.[20] Certain kinds of articles and certain manners of writing were already familiar. In this connection one has only to think of Lamb and Hazlitt to gain an idea of the best sort of journalism practiced in this period.

To the gallery of journalistic types that already included the critic, the reporter, the humorist, the writer of memoirs, the political commentator, De Quincey added a new character—the popularizing scholar. One can trace the development of this type through the sequence of his early writings. In his first and most famous publication, *The Confessions of an English Opium Eater*, a work that bears the significant subtitle, "An Extract from the Life of a Scholar," De Quincey appeared before the public as an eccentric but profound student of matters of intellectual interest. In making his confessions, he presented as the pleasures of opium those satisfactions and pursuits that are identified with the intellectual character—the appreciation of fine music, the study of philosophy, and the imaginative exercises of the mind in reveries and fantasies. And, as has been seen, when he attempted to continue his career in the pages of *The London Magazine*, the topics that most naturally occurred to him were products of his own scholarly interests —translations from the German, criticisms of economic theorists, and investigations into such recondite questions as the origin of the Rosicrucians and the Freemasons. Being new to the craft, in these early papers he was not especially fortunate in his choice of topics. In later years, working along the same lines, he did much better, and developed a successful formula for writing scholarly articles directed to a popular audience.

The new magazine-reading public was eager for a taste of high culture and erudition. It was no longer a small public trained up in the classics, but rather a large and vaguely defined mass of readers who, though not enjoying the advantages of a classical education, were still interested in some learning. De Quincey must have realized that he could capitalize on his scholarly manner, his refined and exquisite tastes, his extensive reading in out-of-the-way books, and his extreme sophistication of attitude. His self-consciousness was always great, and he must have known perfectly well what he was about when he presented himself, as he invariably did, as a very strange and superior sort of man. If, as is here being suggested, his manner became something of a pose, it was perhaps principally because he was always so intent upon presenting the side of himself that would be most interesting to his audience.

He had, however, to dramatize not only himself but also the matter that he was going to impart. And so he adopted the practice of presenting every discussion as the dramatic revelation of some new discovery, which, issuing from a mind untrammeled by learned prejudices, was naturally superior to what had been previously done with the subject by academic scholars. And so in article after article, one finds him commencing by disparaging previous treatments of his theme or by proclaiming that nothing had yet been done with his subject, thus suggesting that what was to follow was not only sound and informative, but novel and even revolutionary. In addition, he displayed great skill in giving what was merely a popular exposition the appearance of a scholarly treatise replete with Greek and Latin quotations and impressive allusions to foreign authorities. At the same time, his painstaking clarity of exposition and felicity in the use of illustration made the most elaborate and difficult conceptions easily accessible to his untrained and unsophisticated readers. Nor did he neglect the advantage to be gained from subjects that had an air of mystery or the glamor of the esoteric. His preference for remote periods and strange events was not only a reflection of his own romantic nature; it was also in part determined by his sense of what would interest the public.

To the ordinary reader—the reader whom De Quincey had in mind when writing—his expositions of scholarly, historical, and philosophical themes were original and enlightening. De Quincey could not forbear claiming for his work a value in excess of its actual merit; but judged in respect to the purpose that it was intended to serve, it was often extremely good. The difficulty arises when one takes his pretensions at their face value, or when one infers, from his legitimate achievements, powers and capacities that he did not actually possess. If one looks upon him as essentially a journalist with extraordinary stylistic ability, a remarkable talent for description, and a lively imaginative sense of scholarship and all things intellectual, one has taken a proper measure of his abilities and arrived at an accurate estimate of the majority of his works. But to think of him as a consistently original mind in the province of either art or thought is to confuse illusion with reality.

Notes / Bibliography / Index

NOTES

Throughout the text and notes references to *The Collected Writings of Thomas De Quincey*, ed. David Masson, 14 vols. (London, 1897) will be indicated only by volume and page number.

CHAPTER I *The Background*

1. David Masson, *Thomas De Quincey* (London, 1881), pp. 136–40.
2. *De Quincey's Writings*, published by Ticknor, Reed and Fields (Boston, 1851–59), *Confessions*, p. ix. (This edition was printed, for the most part, from the original magazine versions of De Quincey's papers, and reference will be made to it whenever the passage or particular version of the passage quoted was omitted in the author's revision and therefore is not to be found in the standard edition.)
3. *Ibid.*, p. 18.
4. R. P. Gillies, *Memoirs of a Literary Veteran*, 3 vols. (London, 1851), II, 220.
5. *De Quincey and His Friends: Personal Recollections, Souvenirs, and Anecdotes*, ed. James Hogg (London, 1895), pp. 73–74.
6. "His display of omniscience, the pontifical tone, the constant self-congratulations, the mysterious hints of enormous hidden knowledge on faraway subjects . . . are not only temperamental failings, but must be explained by conformity to the tone of the magazines for which De Quincey wrote and the hopes which he had to raise in editors and readers." René Wellek, "De Quincey's Status in the History of Ideas," *PQ*, XXIII (July, 1944), 271.

7. Oliver Elton, *A Survey of English Literature: 1780–1830*, 2 vols. (London, 1924), II, 2. 313.

8. Horace Ainsworth Eaton, *Thomas De Quincey: A Biography* (New York, 1936), p. 353.

9. Alone among students of De Quincey, Oliver Elton seems to have divined the truth: "[De Quincey] was capable of taking some dull or remote authority, saying nothing about it, and dressing it out, without scruple, for the readers of his journal." (*op. cit.*, II, 316). It is odd, though, that the only example of this practice which Elton cites should be the article on the Essenes, probably one of the few exceptions to the rule. See Chapter II.

10. *Selections, Grave and Gay, from the Writings, Published and Unpublished, of Thomas De Quincey, Revised and Arranged by Himself*, 14 vols. Published by James Hogg (Edinburgh, 1853–60).

11. Joseph A. Sandhaas, "De Quincey's *Revolt of the Tartars* Seen in the Light of Chinese, French, German and English Source Material" (Unpublished Ph.D. dissertation, Boston University, 1946). Erhart H. Essig, "Thomas De Quincey and Robert Pearse Gillies as Champions of German Literature and Thought" (Unpublished Ph.D. dissertation, Northwestern University, 1951). The findings of these studies will be discussed and evaluated in the sequel.

12. The following are a few examples of the doubts that have been expressed concerning De Quincey's veracity, especially in the *Confessions*.

a] In its review of the Confessions (January, 1824), *The North American Review* states: "We are sometimes in doubt whether what is stated apparently as narrative, is not meant for brilliant fiction, or at least for 'fiction founded on fact.' " H. A. Page (pseudonym for A. H. Japp), *Thomas De Quincey: his Life and Writings*, 2 vols. (London, 1877), I, 239.

b] George Saintsbury remarks, "Many of the details of the *Confessions* and the *Autobiography* have a singular unbelievableness as one reads them; and though the tendency of recent biographers has been to accept them as on the whole genuine, I own that I am rather sceptical about many of them still. Was the ever-famous Malay a real Malay? etc." "De Quincey," *Essays in English Literature*, 2 vols. (London, 1923), I, 212–13.

c] Even more "recent biographers" are apt to sound rather

defensive when treating this question. Professor Eaton, for instance, writes: "the question of De Quincey's accuracy, or even veracity, needs a word. He was a literary artist rather than a reporter. If Thomas Poole asserted that his conversation with De Quincey concerning the Pythagorean saying anent beans was made up out of whole cloth; if, as Dykes Campbell maintains, it is unlikely that Coleridge confessed his opium excesses to the young stranger on their first meeting; the fact is that Coleridge *did* borrow [ideas] without acknowledgment and deny it; and that he was a slave to opium." Eaton, *op. cit.*, p. 359.

13. The following sketch of De Quincey's life is based on a study of the primary materials: the autobiographical writings, the letters, the Diary, the Blackwood Magazine MSS., and the memoirs of De Quincey's friends and acquaintances. However, as the treatment is summary and no controversial issues are raised, the text has been freed from the embarrassment of frequent citations by adopting the following method: when a statement can be conveniently verified by a reference to De Quincey's writings, it has been introduced into the text along with the volume and page number from the standard edition; when there is no citation of any sort, verification can be found in the relevant passage in Eaton's standard life.

14. "This we happen to recollect; having written a tragedy in our 13th year on a certain Ethelfrid—a Caesar Borgia sort of person—who cut the throats of the abbot and all his monks." "Walladmor: Sir Walter Scott's German Novel," The London Magazine, (October, 1824), 363, n.

15. A Diary of Thomas De Quincey, 1803, ed. Horace A. Eaton (New York, 1927).

16. Ibid., p. 182.

17. Horace Ainsworth Eaton, "The Letters of De Quincey to Wordsworth 1803–1807," ELH, III (1936), 15–30.

18. Dr. Cotton, the Provost of Worcester College, stated in later years that De Quincey's reading "had never been conducted upon that system which the Oxford examinations, essentially and very properly intended for men of average abilities, render almost incumbent upon every candidate for the highest honours. De Quincey seems to have felt that he was deficient in that perfect mastery of the minuter details of logic, ethics, and rhetoric, which the practice of the schools demanded." De Quincey and His Friends, p. 109.

19. There was no real interest in German Literature in England until about 1790; and even then it was confined primarily to *Werther, Die Räuber,* Bürger's *Lenore,* the dramas of Kotzebue, and the sensational *Ritter-Räuber-und Schauerromane* popularized by Matthew Gregory ("Monk") Lewis. The fad ended abruptly around 1799, and it was many years before a new and more serious interest was aroused by the efforts of Gillies, De Quincey, and Carlyle. As late as 1806 Gillies had difficulty finding one competent teacher of German. There were a few students of German philosophy, notably Coleridge, but an interest in German scholarship such as DeQuincey records must have been a most unusual phenomenon. See V. Stockley, *German Literature as Known in England 1750–1830* (London, 1929); F. W. Stockoe, *German Influence in the English Romantic Period* (Cambridge, 1926); Erhart H. Essig, *op. cit.*

20. "In 1821 . . . I went up to London avowedly for the purpose of exercising my pen, as the one sole source then open to me for extricating myself from a special embarrassment (failing which case of dire necessity, I believe that I should never had written a line for the press)."—*Collected Writings,* III, 127.

21. *The Convention of Cintra,* octavo pamphlet printed by Longman, Hurst, Rees, and Orme (London, 1809), in *The Prose Works of William Wordsworth,* ed. Rev. Alexander B. Grosart (London, 1876), I, 31–174.

22. In a letter to Catherine Clarkson, April 11, 1815, Dorothy Wordsworth writes, "Mr. De Quincey, notwithstanding his learning and his talents, can do nothing; he is eaten up by the spirit of procrastination; but if once in two or three years he actually does make an effort, he is so slow a labourer that no one who knows him would wish to appoint him to it." *Letters of William and Dorothy Wordsworth, The Middle Years,* ed. Ernest de Selincourt (Oxford, 1937), p. 665.

23. "[De Quincey] has a small independent fortune, and the only thing he wants is a magnificent library; this he is willing to purchase by giving for it a few years' close attention to the law. . . . I represented to him that I feared *nothing* could be expected from the law so studied. A man must be altogether or not at all a lawyer." *Henry Crabb Robinson on Books and Their Writers,* 3 vols., ed. Edith J. Morley (London, 1938), I, 104.

24. Eaton, *Thomas De Quincey: A Biography* (New York, 1936), p. 250.
25. *Close Commentary upon a Straggling Speech*, an octavo pamphlet of 16 pp. printed by Airey and Bellingham, Kendal, 1818. See John Edwin Wells, "Wordsworth and De Quincey in Westmoreland Politics, 1818," *PMLA*, LV (December, 1940), 1080–1128.
26. Charles Pollitt, *De Quincey's Editorship of the Westmoreland Gazette* (Kendal, 1890), pp. 29–30.
27. *Ibid.*, pp. 30–31.
28. "If Wilson and Lockhart do not put themselves forward for the Mag. I foresee that the entire weight of supporting it must rest on my shoulders: I see clearly that I must be its Atlas. . . . a more dreary collection of dullness and royal stupidity never did this world see gathered together than the December No. exhibits. . . . No, no! I see clearly that I must write it all myself." Eaton, *Thomas De Quincey: A Biography*, p. 266.
29. "He was . . . the most talked-of man among the contributors to *The London Magazine* because of the sensational effect of the *Confessions*." *Ibid.*, p. 279.
30. J. R. Findlay describes De Quincey's conversation in these words. "He did not quite, as Burton had told me he would do, talk magazine articles, but the literary habit was notable . . . when in the flow of his conversation he came to the close of one of his beautifully rounded and balanced paragraphs, he would pause in order to allow you to have your say. . . . The listener was apt to feel that he had perorated rather than paused." *De Quincey and His Friends*, pp. 127–28.
31. Edward Sackville-West, *Thomas De Quincey* (New Haven, 1936), p. 142.
32. "In order to excuse the tone (which occasionally I may be obliged to assume) of one speaking as from a station of knowledge to others having no knowledge, I beg it to be understood that I take that station deliberately, on no conceit of superiority to my readers, but as a companion adapting my services to the wants of those who need them."—X, 365.
33. "Notes of Conversations with Thomas De Quincey by Richard Woodhouse," *De Quincey and His Friends*, p. 77.
34. *Malthus on Population* (IX, 11–19).
35. Hazlitt's letter begins, "Sir—Will you have the kindness to insert in the "Lion's Head" the two following passages from

a work of mine published some time since? They exhibit a rather striking coincidence with the reasonings of the 'Opium Eater' in your late number on the discoveries of Mr. Malthus; and as I have been a good deal abused for my skepticism on that subject, I do not feel quite disposed that any one else should run away with the credit of it. I do not wish to bring any charge of plagiarism in this case: I only beg to put in my own claim of priority."—IX, 20. For De Quincey's reply see IX, 23–31.

36. As the extent of De Quincey's intellectual indebtedness to Wordsworth has never been fully assessed, and as this study is concerned in part with demonstrating the derivative nature of De Quincey's thought, it seems appropriate to present the evidence of his dependency.

a] The Literature of Knowledge and the Literature of Power.

This distinction first appears in "Letters to a Young Man whose Education has been neglected," 1823. See X, 48 and the note which reads, "For which distinction, as for most of the sound criticism on poetry, or any subject connected with it that I have ever met with, I must acknowledge my obligations to many years' conversation with Mr. Wordsworth."

The distinction was further elaborated in "The Poetry of Pope," 1848. See XI, 53–60.

The term "power," so central to De Quincey's critical vocabulary, was evidently a favorite word with Wordsworth, though he does not employ it in his critical writings. "Walked to Hampstead. Found Wordsworth demonstrating to Hammond some of the points of his philosophical theory. Speaking of his own poems, he said he valued them principally as being a new power in the literary world." (May 31, 1812.) *Henry Crabb Robinson on Books and Their Writers*, I, 138.

b] Style as the Incarnation of Thought.

See "Language," V, 228–30.

c] Theory of Rhetoric.

Sigmund K. Proctor in his *Thomas De Quincey's Theory of Literature* (Ann Arbor, 1943) argues that De Quincey's most original contribution to esthetics is his theory of rhetoric. See chapter VI.

Wordsworth read De Quincey's "Rhetoric" (X, 81–133) and communicated his impressions to Henry Crabb Robinson. "In the same number of *Blackwood* is an article upon "Rhetoric," undoubtedly from De Quincey. . . . There are in it some things from my Conversation—which the Writer does not seem aware of." (Jan. 27, 1829), *The Correspondence of Henry Crabb Robinson with the Wordsworth Circle (1808-1866)*, 2 vols., ed. Edith J. Morley (Oxford, 1927), I, 201.

d] Definition of the Picturesque.

The picturesque De Quincey defines brilliantly in a long note (II, 360–61) to his description of Dove Cottage. In another essay he remarks of Wordsworth that "there were fields of thought or of observation which he seemed to think locked up and sacred to himself. . . . One of these, and which naturally occurred the most frequently, was the whole theory of picturesque beauty."—III, 198.

e] Ideality of Achilles.

In "Homer and the Homeridae" De Quincey comments at length on the ideality and unity of the character of Achilles as portrayed in the *Iliad*. He acknowledges the idea as Wordsworth's. (VI, 80–81)

f] Review of *Wilhelm Meister*. (XI, 222–58)

De Quincey's denunciation of *Wilhelm Meister* as indecent has always been regarded as an extraordinary instance of critical malice and irresponsibility. He was probably encouraged to take such a strong stand by Wordsworth's reaction to the book. "Among other things he [De Quincey] mentioned that Wordsworth, who was apt to take extreme opinions up on such subjects, regarded Goethe as little better than a quack. Wordsworth he said, never read books, but somehow or other 'Wilhelm Meister' had fallen in his way, and he had gone through it till he came to the scene where the hero, in his mistress's [*sic*] bedroom, becomes sentimental over her dirty towels, etc., which struck him with such disgust that he flung the book out of his hand, would never look at it again, and declared that no English lady would ever read such a work." "Personal Recollections by John Ritchie Findlay," *De Quincey and His Friends*, p. 144. See De Quincey. "Even from personal uncleanliness Mr. Goethe thinks it possible to derive a grace . . . the highest scene of this nature is the bedroom of Mariana: it passes all belief; 'Combs, soap, towels, *with the traces of their use*, were not concealed.' "—XI, 234.

37. A Scottish legal term signifying the public denunciation of a recalcitrant debtor. See Eaton, *Thomas De Quincey: A Biography*, pp. 341–42.

38. "For the last 15 or 16 days, having a family of 12 persons absolutely dependent upon me . . . for mere daily necessities of warmth—light—food, etc., by daily sales of books at the rate of about 30s. for 1s. In that proportion have been my sacrifices; and I have now literally no more to sacrifice that could be saleable." (Letter of 1833, *ibid.*, p. 344). ". . . having in a moment of pinching difficulty for my children about 10 months since pawned every article of my dress which would produce a shilling, I have since that time had no stockings, no shoes, no neck handkerchief, coat, waistcoat, or hat. I have sat constantly barefoot; and, being constitutionally or from the use of opium unusually sensible of cold, I should really have been unable to sit up and write but for a counterpane which I wrap around my shoulders." (Letter of May 22, 1840, *Blackwood's Magazine* MS 4038). "I really know not which way to turn. And when I look on the books—hardly 6 through the last 5 years that I have had, my wonder is—how I have kept afloat at all." (Letter of 1842, Eaton, *Thomas De Quincey: A Biography*, p. 402.

39. Letter to Professor Nichol (1844) in H. A. Page, *op. cit.*, I, 325.

40. Letter of 1846 in Page, *op. cit.*, I, 340.

CHAPTER II *The Polyhistor*

1. *Collected Writings*, IV, 118–239.
2. Edward Sackville-West, *Thomas De Quincey* (New Haven, 1936), p. 203.
3. IV, 118 n.
4. "The Bishop of Gloucester [Dr. Monk], who gives the fullest materials yet published for a just decision [on Bentley's character], leaves us to collect it for ourselves."—IV, 121.
5. John Lockhart complained about the practice of reviewers: "An English Reviewer is a smart, clever man of the world, or else a violent political zealot. He takes up a new book either to make a jest of it, and amuse his readers and himself at the expense of its author, or he makes use of the name of it merely as an excuse for writing, what he thinks the author might have been better employed in doing. . . . The truth is, that the English Reviewer does not much care what the merit of the author is. The author is a mere puppet in the hands of the critic . . . the author is nothing—the Reviewer

everything." "Remarks on the Periodical Criticism of England—in a Letter to a Friend," *Lockhart's Literary Criticism,* ed. M. Clive Hildyard (Oxford, 1931), p. 59.

6. The following are some examples of De Quincey's treatment of Dr. Monk. "Of all biographers, Dr. Monk is the most perversely obscure in fixing dates."—IV, 179. "This passage, therefore, in mere prudence, Dr. Monk will cancel in his next edition: in fact, I cannot conceive how such a mistake [in reading a Greek passage] has arisen with a man of his learning."—IV, 133. "He [Monk] certainly thinks too highly of Colbatch, the most persevering of all Bentley's enemies, and a malicious old toad. If that, however, be Dr. Monk's leaning, there are others (with avenues, perhaps as good, to secret information) whose bias was the other way."—IV, 121. "Dr. Monk lays down the orthodox morality on this subject [Bentley's birth], in a way not at all surpassed by the copy-head of any possible writing-master."—IV, 126.

7. Monk, p. 347. The only point in which De Quincey's account is independent of Monk's is in his estimate of Bentley's character. And here he has drastically simplified and distorted the careful and judicious conclusions of his precursor. In speaking of the problem of estimating Bentley's character, Monk writes as follows: "Having spared no pains investigating the truth, by reference to authentic documents, and by comparison of opposite accounts from different parties, I am in hopes that I have generally succeeded in giving a faithful representation of the facts; but while I endeavor to do justice to Dr. Bentley, it is frequently necessary to exhibit his conduct in an unfavourable light, and such as reflects no credit upon his character, station, or profession."—*ibid.,* p. ix. With this reserved but firm assertion of the rights of truth, compare De Quincey's language on the same question: "I would propose that at this time of day Bentley should be pronounced right, and his enemies utterly in the wrong . . . for by this means the current of one's sympathy with an illustrious man is cleared of ugly obstructions, and enabled to flow unbroken." —IV, 121.

8. An example of De Quincey's minute knowledge of Bentley's writings is provided by the following: "In the same year Bentley wrote a letter to Biel upon the scriptural glosses in our present copies of Hesychius, which he considered interpolations from a later hand. This letter . . . has been published by

Alberti in the Prolegomena to his edition of that lexicographer."—IV, 185–86.

Compare with Monk: "A specimen of our critic's insight into Hesychius was called forth by a correspondence with John Christian Biel, a divine of Brunswick, best known by his posthumous work, the Thesaurus of the Old Testament. He was then preparing for publication a collection of all the scriptural glosses found in Hesychius; but having some time before travelled in England, where he visited the Universities, and was received by our Aristarchus with the kindness which he never failed to extend to scholars, and remembered to have learned from him, that those explanations of scriptural expressions were not Hesychius's, but interpolated in his Lexicon by some later hand. He therefore wrote to enquire the grounds of this opinion, and received from Bentley, in reply, a very full and clear demonstration of this phenomenon. Bentley's letter, which is not only learned, but amusing, was communicated by Biel to Alberti, and printed among his Prolegomena."—Monk, pp. 317–18.

De Quincey's familiarity with the circumstances that occasioned Bentley's work may also be traced to Monk; for example, De Quincey writes: "In July 1696, on taking his doctor's degree, Bentley maintained three separate theses: one 'On the Rationality of the Mosaic Cosmogony and Deluge'; a second 'On the Divine Origin of the Christian Miracles'; and a third 'On the Relation between the Christian and Platonic Trinities.' . . . On the Sunday following he preached before the university what is called the Commencement Sermon ('Of Revelation and the Messiah'). Many years afterwards, this was added as an appropriate sequel to an edition of his Boyle Lectures in 1692. It is a powerful and learned (however imperfect) defence of the Christian faith, and of its founder's claim to the character of the Jewish Messiah."—IV, 178–79.

Compare with Monk: "In July 1696 Bentley was created Doctor of Divinity at Cambridge. As his exercise for this degree, he was appointed to keep the 'Public Act' at the Commencement; a theological disputation which formerly constituted the principal object of interest at that solemnity. . . . The three subjects defended by Bentley on this occasion were: 1. The Mosaic account of the creation and the deluge; 2. The proof of divine authority by the miracles recorded in Scripture; 3. The identity of the Christian and Platonic Trinity. . . .

Our new Doctor was likewise appointed to preach before the University on the Commencement Sunday. His discourse was a defense of revelation against the deists, and a proof that the Author of our Religion was the Messiah; a subject which he treated with his characteristic ability, perspicuity, and closeness of reasoning. It was printed at the time; and being added, many years afterwards, to an edition of his Boyle's Lectures, it continues to be read and valued as one of the most powerful vindications of Christianity from the cavils of infidels." [A note gives the title as 'Of Revelation and the Messias.'] (Monk, p. 57.)

9. As a reviewer, De Quincey was not usually captious or vituperative. In a review of Thomas Gordon's *The Revolution of Greece* (Edinburgh, 1833)—an elaborate summary like the "Bentley" piece—he makes a full acknowledgment of his intention and generously praises the author. "Mr. Gordon, of forty authors who have partially treated this theme, is the first who can be considered either impartial or comprehensive; and upon his authority, not seldom using his words, we shall now present to our readers the first continuous abstract of this most interesting and romantic war."—VII, 286. De Quincey's harsh treatment of Monk is most likely explained by the nature of the subject: themes of classical scholarship always aroused De Quincey to bellicose assertions of authority and to fierce attacks on those whom he took to be his rivals in the field. His own pretensions were astonishing; he once told Crabb Robinson that he was "the second Greek scholar in the kingdom." *Henry Crabb Robinson on Books and Their Writers*, 3 vols., ed. Edith J. Morley (London, 1938), I, 195.

10. IV, 237–87.

11. John E. Jordan, *Thomas De Quincey Literary Critic* (Berkeley, 1952), p. 155.

12. The parade of authorities commences on the first page. "Dr. Johnson, however, and Joseph Warton, for reasons not stated, have placed his birth on the 22d. To this statement, as opposed to that which comes from the personal friends of Pope, little attention is due. Ruffhead and Spence, upon such questions, must always be of higher authority than Johnson and Warton, and a *fortiori* than Bowles. But it ought not to be concealed, though hitherto unnoticed by any person, that some doubt after all remains whether any of the biographers is right." —IV, 237.

13. *The Works of Alexander Pope, Esq.*, ed. William Roscoe, 10 vols. (London, 1824).

14. *Ibid.*, I, 12.

15. *Ibid.*, I, 281.

16. The full and proper title of the *Sketches* is *Sketches of Men and Manners from the Autobiography of an English Opium Eater.* The series ran in *Tait's Edinburgh Magazine* from 1834 to 1840, a few papers appearing each year. Masson rearranged this material and printed it under the title *Autobiography* in Vols. I and II of the standard edition.

17. Sackville-West says about the "Autobiographic Sketches": "these sketches, fascinating as they are, have not the concentration—the peculiar intensity—of the *Confessions.* . . . They are too diffuse, too casual, too much encumbered with asides." *Op. cit.*, p. 195.

18. "First Irish Rebellion of 1798" (I, 227–48); "French Invasion of Ireland and Second Rebellion of 1798" (I, 249–66).

19. "I in particular was led, by hearing on every side the conversation reverting to the dangers and tragic incidents of the era, separated from us by not quite two years, to make inquiries of everybody who had personally participated in the commotions."—I, 249.

20. "As to the Rebellion in Ireland, the English, I think, use *the amplifying,* and the Irish *the diminishing Hyperbole;* . . . In England I remember, we heard such horrid accounts of Murders and Battles and Robberies, and here . . . they affect to treat [the Rebellion] with Indifference, and speak of it as we should of a Birmingham riot." Horace Ainsworth Eaton, *Thomas De Quincey: A Biography* (New York, 1936), pp. 46–47.

21. Rev. James Gordon, *History of the Rebellion in Ireland in the Year 1798, etc. containing an impartial account of the proceedings of The Irish Revolutionists, From the Year 1782, till the Suppression of the Rebellion* (London, 1803). A novel by Michael Banim, *The Croppy: A Tale of 1798* (London, 1828) was also based on Gordon's history. In the preface to the reprint of 1866 Banim writes, "The best book I could find referring to the Wexford outbreaks was one published by the Rev. Mr. Gordon, a Protestant Clergyman."—p. iii.

22. Gordon, pp. 60–61.

23. *A Narrative of what passed at Killala in the County of Mayo and the parts adjacent during the French Invasion in the Sum-*

mer of 1798. By an *Eyewitness* (London, 1800). The pamphlet is an anonymous publication, but Gordon identifies the
author as Dr. Joseph Stock. Gordon's excerpts from this pamphlet are found in his book between p. 305 and p. 343.
24. IV, 395–421.
25. See V. R., "De Quincey: Some Objections and Corrections," *Notes and Queries*, CCXXIX (1940), 433.
26. IV, 422–39. This is not the only occasion when the inadequacy of De Quincey's knowledge made him limp feebly off the
field. His article on the great German historian Barthold Georg
Niebuhr (published in the May, 1841, issue of *Blackwood's*)
concludes: "Of his great work, *Roman History*, so far as it is
completed, we shall only say this—that before any sound criticism can be applied to it, we must see it well analyzed. At present it is a pile of materials, not an edifice; and the most embarrassed in its plan of any work we know."
27. Heinrich Doering, *Friederich von Schiller's Leben* (Weimar, 1822).
28. In einem noch vorhandenen eigenen Aufsatze äussert er sich
darüber auf eine herzliche, rührend fromme Weise: "Und du
Wesen aller Wesen! Dich hab' ich nach der Geburt meines
einzigen Sohnes gebeten, dass du demselben an Geistesstärke
zulegen möchtest, was ich aus Mangel an Unterricht nicht er-
reichen konnte, und du hast mich erhört. Dank Dir, gütigstes
Wesen, dass du auf die Bitten der Sterblichen achtest!" *Ibid.*,
p. 5. Doering's life was included in most of the early editions
of Schiller's works, and as De Quincey had such an edition in
his possession at one time, I think it possible that he may have
preserved a few memoranda. De Quincey writes in a letter of
1819: "Mr. Murray, the publisher, sent me a work for reviewal
four months ago (the entire works of Schiller in 26 vols.)"
H. A. Page (pseudonym for A. H. Japp), *Thomas De Quincey:
His Life and Writings*, 2 vols. (London, 1877), I, 207.
29. "Goethe as reflected in his Novel of Wilhelm Meister."
(XI, 222–58) Of the *Wallenstein* De Quincey wrote, "Even
Schiller's fine drama of Wallenstein, as it appears in English
dress, is indebted for all its splendors to the admirable genius
of its translator, Mr. Coleridge." Charles Pollitt, *De Quincey's
Editorship of the Westmoreland Gazette* (Kendal, 1890), p.
29.
30. "[The narrative has] as much of a personal interest in the
moving characters, with fine dramatic contracts, as belongs to

'Venice Preserved,' or to the 'Fiesco' of Schiller."—VII, 369.

31. IV, 17–85.

32. IV, 17 n.

33. *The Dramatic Works of William Shakespeare*, ed. Thomas Thomas Campbell (London, 1866).

34. The *Encyclopaedia* articles on Goethe, Schiller, and Shakespeare round out the series of De Quincey's formal lives, with the exception of the brief life of Milton he wrote for Charles Knight's series of biographies, *Distinguished Men of Modern Times*. (IV, 86–103) From its compressed and circumstantial style, its obvious familiarity with the materials for Milton's life, and its rigorous organization, the essay on Milton suggests a derivation similar to that of the lives of Bentley and Pope. However, the source has not been located, although all the lives of Milton with which De Quincey may have been familiar have been examined. It is possible, of course, that he could have derived his materials from a source such as an encyclopaedia article. In any case, there is no reason to suppose that this paper forms an exception to the practice he so consistently employed.

35. VII, 44–100; VI, 179–224.

36. In this article, De Quincey vaguely alludes to a great many authorities. But on the two occasions when he mentions van Brouwer, he quotes him, which signifies actual knowledge of his book and not mere hearsay. The first allusion is rather oblique: "Scepticism naturally courts the patronage of France; and in effect that same remark which a learned Belgian (van Brouwer) has found frequent occasion to make upon single sections of Fontenelle's work may be fairly extended into a representative account of the whole—'*L'on trouve les mêmes arguments chez Fontenelle, mais dégagés des longueurs du savant Van Dale, et exprimés avec plus d'élégance.*' "—VII, 52.

The only other allusion to van Brouwer occurs thirty pages later, buried in a mass of classical citations; but it is even more suggestive. "Brouwer, the Belgic scholar, who has so recently and so temperately treated these subjects ('Histoire de la Civilisation Morale et Religieuse chez les Grecs.' 6 tomes: Groningue, 1840), alleges a case (which, however, I do not remember to have met) where the client ventured to object:— '*Mon roi Appolon, je crois que tu es fou.*' "—VII, 81.

37. De Quincey introduces Abeken into his discussion simply as the most recent student of Cicero. After quoting a short

passage from him which De Quincey concedes contains "a glimpse of the truth which has been so constantly obscured by historians," the German scholar is summarily dismissed: "with the natural incapacity for practical politics which besieges all Germans, he [Abeken] fails in most of the subordinate cases to decipher the intrigues."—VI, 190.

38. "Examen des réponses données par les oracles . . . —sur les oracles qui semblent contenir un conseil ou la confirmation d'une question.—Oracles contenant des preuves internes de leur fausseté.—Oracles dont l'accomplissement peut être attribué au hasard.—Oracles qui, par la manière dont ils étoient rédigés, étoient garantis d'un démenti par l'événement.— Oracles dont l'accomplissement est dû à la connaissance qu'avoient les prêtres des circonstances et du caractère des consultants." van Brouwer, III, 233.

39. "Je n'hésite pas à ajouter qu'il me paroît qu'en général les oracles se rangeoient du côté de l'humanité, des bonnes moeurs, de la vertu, en un mot, tant civic qu'individuelle, et que par conséquent ils ont exercé une influence salutaire sur la civilisation morale des Grecs." *Ibid.*, p. 312.

40. "The unique Delphic oracle—with what great benefits it endowed Greece! Many a tyrant and evil-doer was singled out by its divine voice while it rejected them in pronouncing their fate. Not less important, it has saved many an unfortunate person, advised many without resources, strengthened many a good institution with divine authority, made known many an inspired work of art of the muse which reached it, and hallowed maxims of morality as well as principles of politics." ("Das einzige delphische Orakel, wie grossen Nutzen hat es in Griechenland gestiftet! So manchen Tyrannen und Bösewicht ziechnete seine Götterstimme aus, indem sie ihm abweisend sein Schicksal sagte; nicht minder hat es viele Unglückliche gerettet, so manchen Ratlosen beraten, manche gute Anstalt mit göttlichem Ansehen bekräftigt, so manches Werk der Kunst der Muse, das zu ihm gelangte, bekannt gemacht, und Sittensprüche sowohl als Staatsmaximen geheiligt.") Johann Gottfried Herder, "Ideen zur Philosophie der Geschichte der Menschheit," *Herders Werke*, ed. Prof. Dr. Theodor Matthias, 4 vols. (Leipzig, n.d.), IV, 127–28.

41. Preparing to escape from a rapacious landlord in Edinburgh, a Mr. McIndoe, De Quincey writes to Robert Blackwood, "Now at length, I have a prospect of liberation from the dire

perplexity of my MSS. which only have been the chain of compulsion fettering my free movements." Eaton, *op. cit.*, p. 391.

42. "A series of notes apparently drawn together for the purpose of an article on French drama. They are of interest for the insight they afford into De Quincey's working practices. Each note is a rounded bit of material—an anecdote, an observation, or an argument—some of them are written in a finished style ripe for publication—others are in a (for De Quincey) highly condensed sketchy form." "De Quincey on French Drama," *More Books. The Bulletin of the Boston Public Library* (October, 1939).

43. In March, 1841, De Quincey absconded from Edinburgh, leaving behind most of his possessions but keeping his papers. "The 'papers with a few rare volumes (Giordano Bruno—about 8 separate works, with one almost equally rare) made a load for the porter.'" Eaton, *op. cit*, p. 395.

44. "This series of papers originally appeared in *Blackwood's Edinburgh Magazine* for October and November, 1832, January, 1833, and June, July, and August, 1834." Masson's note in VI, 225.

45. Sackville-West, *op. cit.*, p. 205.

46. "The best of these papers, like the 'Caesars' and the 'Revolt of the Tartars' must be judged rather as works of art than of learning." Oliver Elton, *A Survey of English Literature 1780–1830*, 2 vols. (London, 1924), I, 314.

47. In the very next year, 1834, after the commencement of the "Caesars," De Quincey began his "Autobiographic Sketches," which are likewise anecdotal narratives.

48. "Before he left McIndoe's, De Quincey had sent to Robert Blackwood to keep for him the Augustan History, edited by Salmasius, folio. (Bl. MSS.; 7 June 1841.)" Eaton, *op. cit.*, p. 395 n.

49. The following account is based primarily on David Magie's introduction to the Loeb Classics edition of the *Scriptores Historiae Augustae*, ed. David Magie, 3 vols. (London, 1943).

50. An undated letter in the *Blackwood's Magazine* MSS. shows De Quincey busy copying out the notes from the Augustan History. "I am writing like a fiend to secure the *élite* of the notes in the Augustan Hist.—which book I have twice been obliged to return to the Adv [ocat's] Lib [rary] with slight hope of getting it again." (Bl. MS 4717)

51. Verum minis eius ac violentia territus perdere statuit; et cum ter veneno temptasset sentiretque antidotis praemunitam, lacunaria, quae noctu super dormientem laxata machina deciderent, paravit. Hoc consilio per conscios parum celato solutilem navem, cuius vel naufragio vel camarae ruina periret, commentus est atque ita reconciliatione simulata iucundissimis litteris Baias evocavit ad sollemnia Quinquatruum simul celebranda; datoque negotio trierarchis, qui liburnicam qua advecta erat velut fortuito concursu confringerent, protraxit convivium repetentique Baulos in locum corrupti navigii machinosum illud optulit, hilare prosecutus atque in digressu papillas quoque exosculatus. Reliquum temporis cum magna trepidatione vigilavit opperiens coeptorum exitum. Sed ut diversa omnia nandoque evasisse eam comperit, inops consilii L. Agermum libertum eius salvam et incolumem cum gaudio nuntiantem, abiecto clam iuxta pugione ut percussorem sibi subornatum arripi constringique iussit, matrem occidi, quasi deprehensum crimen voluntaria morte vitasset. Suetonius, *De Vita Caesarum*, ed. and tr. J. C. Rolfe, 2 vols. (London, 1951), II, 143–44.

52. VI, 96–138. First printed in *Blackwood's Edinburgh Magazine*, January, 1842.

53. Sackville-West, *op. cit.*, p. 241.

54. Eaton, *op. cit.*, p. 352.

55. Hermann Bobrik, *Geographie des Herodot* (Königsberg, 1838).

56. De Quincey alludes to Bobrik only twice. The first time is near the beginning of his paper. "Yet, if any man . . . demurs to our revision, as having no special invitation at this immediate moment, then we are happy to tell him that Mr. Hermann Bobrik has furnished us with such an invitation by a recent review of Herodotus as a geographer, and thus furnished even a technical plea for calling the great man up before the bar."—VI, 99–100.

The second allusion is more positive, but far from adequate as acknowledgment. "Mr. Hermann Bobrik is the first torchbearer to Herodotus who has thrown a strong light on his theory of the earth's relation to the solar system."—VI, 113.

57. "Ueber die Geographie Herodots," *Abhandlungen der historisch-philologischen Klasse* (Berlin, 1816), pp. 209–24.

58. *A Dissertation on the Geography of Herodotus*. Tr. from the German of B. G. Niebuhr (Oxford, 1830).

59. "His [Herodotus'] dimensions and distances are so far superior to those of later travellers . . . that Major Rennell, upon a deliberate retrospect of his works, preferred his authority to those who came after him etc."—VI, 109.

60. VI, 7–95. First printed in *Blackwood's Edinburgh Magazine* for October, November, and December, 1841.

61. Eaton, *op. cit.*, p. 400.

62. De Quincey's impressive show of authorities, here as in other instances, is explained by the frequency of such allusions in his sources. From Müller alone he could have learned about Wolff, Heyne, Herder, Nitzsch, and many others.

63. VI, 44, 45–6.

64. "The 'Homer and the Homeridae' . . . has some good points, e.g., in the discovery of the Cretan affinities." V.R., *op. cit.*, 434.

65. VII, 11–43. First published in *Blackwood's Edinburgh Magazine*, December, 1839.

66. "This little piece of literary high spirits can be cordially recommended to those who wish to sample De Quincey at his intolerable worst. The burden of the argument . . . is buried in a facetious rigmarole, teeming with Latin and Greek phrases, mixed together, pudding-fashion, to produce an explosion of feeble puns." Sackville-West, *op. cit.*, p. 206.

67. In the course of the investigation, testimony is exacted from Galen, Augustus Caesar, Salmasius, Pliny the Younger, Seneca, Cicero, the Emperor Hadrian, Juvenal, and Isidore of Seville!

68. *Scriptores Historiae Augustae Cum integris Notis Isaaci Casauboni, Cl. Salmasii & Jani Gruteri*, 2 vols. (Leyden, 1671), II, 614–16 n.

69. For De Quincey's use of Salmasius' notes, see note 51, this chapter.

70. "Discursiveness, a major flaw in romantic literature, is De Quincey's besetting fault as a writer. He cannot resist the temptation to divagate. The flood-gates of erudition are always ready to burst open; and then he is swept far off his course into inlets and swamps of learning and argument." *A Literary History of England*, ed. Albert C. Baugh (New York, 1948), p. 1191. "His counterbalancing faults are, indeed, not small. The greatest of them all must, indeed, force itself upon almost any reader who has been gifted with, or has acquired, any critical faculty. It is what has been called, in words not easy

to better, 'an unconquerable tendency to rigmarole.' . . . He does not even wait for fresh game to cross the track of his original and proper quarry: he is constantly and deliberately going out of his way to seek and start it right and left." George Saintsbury, *The Cambridge History of English Literature*, 15 vols. (Cambridge, Eng., 1907–16), XII, 227–28.

71. "But there are four evil qualities . . . which begin to consolidate themselves—to preponderate dismayingly—in the writings of the second period: Pedantry, Digression, Prolixity, and Facetiousness. These bad fairies were present at De Quincey's birth, and they may be said to have been largely successful in encompassing his ruin; for, if the bulk of his work is so little read today, the responsibility must be laid at their door." Sackville-West, *op. cit.*, p. 190.

72. "His interlined and laden-margined MSS indicate that, despite the circumstances, he wrote meticulously, striving for perfection of phrase: 'here, as always,' he says in a letter of 1851, 'I have written my best.' " Jordan, *op. cit.*, p. 15. To comprehend how much labor of revision De Quincey invested in his writings, one must study the *Blackwood's Magazine* Manuscripts, 300-odd letters from De Quincey to his editor and publisher. Almost everything submitted was returned to him for revision, the condensing, deleting and rewriting of sizable portions being a standard practice. On one or two occasions De Quincey was too ill to revise his own work and the job was undertaken by someone else.

73. IV, 323–79. First published in *Blackwood's Edinburgh Magazine*, February, 1827.

74. Sackville-West, *op. cit.*, pp. 164–65.

75. Königsberg, 1804.

76. "ich den Mann, der auf der grossen Bühne der gelehrten Welt eine Hauptrolle und mit beynahe allgemeine Beyfalle spielte, ohne alle Schminke und entkleidet von allem Prunk, gleichsam nur in seinem Negligee darstelle." *Ibid.*, p. 10.

77. "Meine Bekanntschaft mit ihm, entstand nicht in seiner letzten Lebenszeit, und mit ihm vertraut zu werden, dazu gehörte mehr, als Ein Jahrzehend. In den Jahren drey oder vier und Siebenzig (genau weiss ich es nicht) wurde ich sein Zuhörer und später hin sein Amanuensis; durch welches letztere Verhältniss ich dann auch mit ihm in eine nähere Verbindung kam, als seine übrigen Zuhörer. Er gestattete mir

unentgeltlich ohne meine Bitte das Besuchen seines Hörsaals."
Ibid., p. 16.

78. "Das schon oft erwähnte Landshäuschen liegt auf einer
Anhöhe unter hohen Erlen. Unten im Thale fliesst ein kleiner
Bach mit einem Wasserfall, dessen Rauschen Kant bemerkte.
Diese Parthie erweckte in ihm eine schlummernde Idee, die
sich bis zur grössten Lebhaftigkeit ausbildete. Mit fast poetis-
cher Mahlerey, die Kant sonst in seinen Erzählungen gerne
vermied, schilderte er mir in der Folge das Vergnügen, welches
ein schöner Sommermorgen in den frühern Jahren seines
Lebens ihm auf einem Rittergute, in der dort befindlichen
Gartenlaube an den hohen Ufern der Alle, bey einer Tasse
Kaffe, und einer Pfeife gemacht hatte." *Ibid.,* p. 149.

79. "Durch vieljährige Gewohnheit hatte er eine besondere
Fertigkeit erlangt, sich in die Decken einzuhüllen. Beym
Schlafengehen setzte er sich erst ins Bett, schwang sich mit
Leichtigkeit hinein, zog den einen Zipfel der Decke über die
eine Schulter unter dem Rücken durch bis zur andern und
durch eine besondere Geschicklichkeit auch andern unter sich,
und dann weiter bis auf den Leib. So emballirt und gleichsam
wie ein Cocon eingesponnen, erwartete er den Schlaf." *Ibid.,*
p. 32.

80. I have been able to find only one reference to this paper
in connection with its source. Professor René Wellek remarks,
"De Quincey wrote there [*Blackwood's*] on 'The Last Days of
Immanuel Kant.' The article is mainly taken from E. A. Ch.
Wasianski's 'Immanuel Kant in seinen letzten Lebensjahren.' "
Immanuel Kant in England 1798–1838 (Princeton, 1931), p.
172.

81. VI, 152–78. First published in *Blackwood's Edinburgh
Magazine,* March, 1828.

82. "Sir,—Some years ago you published a translation of
Böttiger's *Sabina,* a learned account of the Roman toilette. I
here send you a companion to that work,—not a direct translation, but a very minute abstract (weeded of that wordiness
which has made the original unreadable, and therefore unread)
from a similar dissertation by Hartmann."—VI, 152.

83. "Certainly Mr. Hartmann has the most excellent gifts at
verbal expansion, and talents the most splendid for tautology,
that ever came within my knowledge; and I have found no
particular difficulty in compressing every tittle of what relates
to his subject into a compass which, I imagine, will fill about

one twenty-eighth part at the utmost of the original work."—
VI, 152–53.

84. Erhart H. Essig, "Thomas De Quincey and Robert Pearse
Gillies as Champions of German Literature and Thought"
(Unpublished Ph.D. dissertation, Northwestern University,
1951).

85. *Ibid*, p. 98.

86. Sackville-West, *op. cit.*, p. 208.

87. It is significant that the first man to reveal Coleridge's
plagiarisms and to explain them as psychological quirks was
De Quincey. In an essay entitled "Samuel Taylor Coleridge:
By the English Opium-Eater" published in *Tait's Edinburgh
Magazine*, September, 1834, De Quincey uncovers four in-
stances of plagiarism, including the much-discussed plagiarisms
from Schelling in the *Biographia Literaria*. (II, 142–47) For
a discussion of Coleridge's plagiarisms see Joseph Warren
Beach, "Coleridge's Borrowings from the German," *ELH*
(March, 1942), 36–58.

88. XIII, 384–448. First published in *The London Magazine*,
January, February, March, and June, 1824.

89. Essig, *op. cit.*, pp. 159–60.

90. Elton, *op. cit.*, II, 316–17.

91. VII, 101–72. First published in *Blackwood's Edinburgh
Magazine*, January, April, and May, 1840.

92. *Genuine Works of Josephus Flavius, the Jewish Historian,
translated from the original Greek, with proper Notes, etc.*
William Whiston (London, 1737). De Quincey quotes from
Whiston's translation repeatedly. See pp. 109—13. For whatever value it may have as confirmation of De Quincey's originality in this instance, here is the first notice of the article in
his correspondence with Blackwood: "I shall send you a paper
on a discovery in relation to the earliest Christians made in
the course of studying Josephus." (Letter of December 13,
1839, *Blackwood's Magazine* MS. 4038).

93. II, 81–109. First published under the title "Autobiography
of an English Opium-Eater continued" in *Tait's Edinburgh
Magazine*, June, 1836.

94. René Wellek, "De Quincey's Status in the History of
Ideas," *P.Q*, XXIII (July, 1944), 178–79.

95. For a very thorough and well-balanced treatment of the
whole question of De Quincey's interpretation of Kant, see:
Peter Michelson, "Thomas De Quincey und die Kantische

Philosophie," *Revue de Littérature Comparée*, XXXIII (1959), 356–75.

CHAPTER III *Rifacimento*

1. Horace Ainsworth Eaton, *Thomas De Quincey: A Biography* (New York, 1936), p. 400. This article was overlooked by Masson and not included in the standard edition. Eaton remarks: "for some reason it seems never to have been printed." Actually, the article appeared in *Blackwood's Edinburgh Magazine*, June, 1841. See William E. A. Axon, "The Canon of De Quincey's Writings," *Transactions of the Royal Society of Literature*, Second Series, XXXII, Pt. I (1913), 1–46.

2. A German publisher named Palm was shot on Napoleon's orders after publishing a book by Arndt which attacked Napoleon.

3. "Ich sah hier unter den mannigfaltigsten und wechselvollsten Gestalten die verschiedenen russischen Völkerschaaren an mir vorbeimarschiren und vorbeigalloppiren, die vom Eismeer und vom Ural her und die in der Wolga und im Schwarzen Meere ihre Rosse tränken, schöne Tataren aus der Kabarda und aus der Krimm, stattliche Kossacken vom Don, Kalmücken mit platten Nasen, bretternen Leibern, schiefen Beinen und schiefen Augen, wie Ammian vor funfzehnhundert Jahren seine Hunnen malt, und Baschkiren mit Bogen und Pfeilen. Aber das Prächtigste war ein Geschwader von einem Fähnlein tscherkessischer Reiter, in Stahlhemden und mit Stahlmützen mit wehenden Federbüschen, schönste schlankste Menschen und schönste Pferde." Ernst Moritz Arndt, *Erinnerungen aus dem Äusseren Leben* (Leipzig, 1840), pp. 137–38.

4. *Blackwood's Edinburgh Magazine* (June, 1841), 742.

5. "Viele zerrissene, zerschlagene, abgedeckte Häuser ohne Menschen und Thiere, nicht einmal eine Katze miaute darin; öde schauerliche Gemäuer und Brandstätten." Arndt, *op. cit.*, p. 171.

6. *Blackwood's*, 755.

7. *Ibid.*, 755–56.

8. "Ich war vor die Stadt gegangen, und hatte mich auf einer grünen Wiese, wo stille Heerden weideten, als wenn kein Krieg wäre, hinter einem Heuhaufen hingestreckt; eine dicht-

lockige Birke wehete über mir, und ich schaute sinnend und träumend in die Welt hinein oder vielmehr in die über mir hinfliessenden Wolken. Siehe! Da tönte Musik in mein Ohr, die immer näher und heller heranklang, und bald rollten mir lange Reihen von Wägen vorüber, die auch Landwehr führten, Geigen und Hornpfeifen auf mehreren Wägen voran, und Ältern, Geschwister, Bräute noch mit. So lustig zog es in den Krieg und in den Tod, gleich einem fantastischen Hochzeittraum, mit Blumen und Spielen an dem Träumenden vorüber." Arndt, *op. cit.*, p. 139.

9. *Blackwood's*, 743–44.

10. *Blackwood's Edinburgh Magazine* (December, 1826), 844–58.

11. *Ibid.*, 857–58. The remark about the gold snuff-box is, I suppose, a sly allusion to the gift Carlyle received from Goethe after the publication of the English translation of *Wilhelm Meister*.

12. The title page reads: "Walladmor. Frei nach dem Englischen des Walter Scott. Von W. . . . Berlin: bei F. A. Herbig. 1824. 3 Bände."

13. "Walladmor: A Pseudo-Waverly Novel," *Collected Writings*, XIV, 132–45.

14. *Erinnerungen von Willibald Alexis*, ed. Max Ewert (Berlin, 1905).

15. W. E. A. Axon, "De Quincey and T. F. Dibden," *The Library*, 1907, p. 268.

16. "Walladmor: Sir Walter Scott's German Novel," *The London Magazine* (October, 1824).

17. H. A. Page (pseudonym for A. H. Japp), *Thomas De Quincey: His Life and Writings*, 2 vols. (London, 1877), I, 262.

18. J. G. Lockhart, *Memoirs of Sir Walter Scott*, 5 vols. (London, 1900), IV, 261.

19. Thomas De Quincey, *Walladmor*, 2 vols. (London, 1825).

20. "Als der junge Mann dies Schloss immer deutlicher und deutlicher erblickte, als die heitere Morgensonne die hellrothen Dächer erleuchtete, und über die hinter dem Schlosse tiefer ins Land steigende, wenn auch winterliche Flur ein freundliches Licht ausgoss, fühlte er eine unbeschreibliche Sehnsucht, und die Lust, hier zu landen, überwog alle Zweifel." Alexis, I, 63.

21. De Quincey, *Walladmor*, I, 81–83.

22. "Unter vielem Zujauchzen der Zuschauer nahten endlich eine Partie Reiter dem Wirtshause, und zwar alle im Schritte und mit möglicher Langsamkeit und Feierlichkeit. Zuerst ritten zwei auf zwei, vier Männer, welche wir Waffenträger nennen wollen, obgleich sich dem fremden Zuschauer die Vermuthung aufdrängen möchte, es seien nur aufgeputzte Stallknechte oder Bediente gewesen. Sie trugen schwarze Jockeijacken, enge lederne Beinkleider, gross Courierstiefeln, und auf den kleinen Hüten Laubzweige." Alexis, I, 184.

23. De Quincey cites this book in a note, *Walladmor*, I, 171; I have not been able to trace it.

24. *Ibid.*

25. "indessen wurde bald darauf an den Schlössern und Eisenriegeln geschoben, das Thor ging auf, und die Reiter sprengten durch den gewölbten Thorweg in einen kleinen, von den Laternen einiger herbeigeeilten alten Dienern erhellten, Hofraum." Alexis, II, 109.

26. De Quincey, *Walladmor*, II, 96–98.

27. De Quincey wrote to Hogg: "Provided that you undertake the narrative portion of the work, I will follow up with the pictorial description." H. A. Page, *op. cit.*, II, 23.

28. Mario Praz, *The Hero in Eclipse in Victorian Fiction*, tr. Angus Davidson (London, 1956), pp. 75–86.

29. See chapter II.

30. II, 403–20. First published in *Tait's Edinburgh Magazine*, June, 1840.

31. *Fragments*, pp. 120–22.

32. "force" is dialectical for a waterfall.

33. "Early Memorials of Grasmere" (XIII, 125–58). First published in *Tait's Edinburgh Magazine*, September, 1839.

34. XIII, 126.

35. *George and Sarah Green. Narrative by Dorothy Wordsworth*, ed. E. de Selincourt (Oxford, 1936). Wordsworth made a ballad on this same subject, viz. "George and Sarah Green." See *The Poetical Works of William Wordsworth*, ed. E. de Selincourt and Helen Darbishire, 5 vols. (Oxford, 1958), IV, 375–76.

36. According to Dorothy Wordsworth's account, the children were snowbound two days, and it was a son of the family, not the eldest girl, who appealed to the neighbors.

37. Dorothy Wordsworth, *op. cit.*, pp. 66–67.

38. "Revolt of the Tartars or, Flight of the Kalmuck Khan and

his People from the Russian Territories to the Frontiers of China." (VII, 368–421)

39. The paper is found in I, 400–27.

40. 2 vols. (Riga, 1804).

41. *Nomadische Streifereien,* I, 139–246.

42. *Voyage de Benjamin Bergmann chez les Kalmuks,* tr. de l'Allemand par M. Morris, Membre de la Societe Asiatique (Chatillon-sur-Seine, 1825).

43. Joseph A. Sandhaas, "De Quincey's *Revolt of the Tartars* Seen in the Light of Chinese, French, German and English Source Material" (Unpublished Ph.D. dissertation, Boston University, 1946).

44. Erhart H. Essig, "Thomas De Quincey and Robert Pearse Gillies as Champions of German Literature and Thought" (Unpublished Ph.D. dissertation, Northwestern University, 1951).

45. Eaton, *op. cit.,* p. 328.

46. De Quincey quotes the Jesuit memoir (VII, 417–18) from the French translation, as can be proved by a comparison of the text of the memoir (which Bergmann translated into German and the French translator put back into French) with the French translation of Bergmann.

47.
German	French	De Quincey
Ubascha	Oubacha	Oubacha
Zaback Dorschi	Zébék-Dorchi	Zebek-Dorchi
Tscherkask	Tcherkask	Tcherkask

48. The principal treatment of the revolt before Bergmann was Peter Simon Pallas, *Sammlungen Historischer Nachrichten über die Mongolischen Völkerschaften,* 2 vols. (St. Petersburg, 1776), I, 60–93. Gibbon discusses the Tartars ("a nation of shepherds and warriors") in *The History of the Decline and Fall of the Roman Empire,* ed. J. B. Bury, 3 vols. (New York, 1946), I, 792–99.

49. "Tels étaient Oubacha et Zébék-Dorchi. Lorsqu'on connaît à fond ces deux caractères, il n'est pas difficile de prévoir la direction que devaient prendre les affaires des kalmuks. Ici franchise et loyauté, là finesse et astuce; ici des idées éloignées de tout mauvais soupçon, là des intrigues qui bouleversant le fond de l'âme; chez celui-ci une confiance trop légère et point de résolution, chez celui-là une trompeuse apparence de justice, et une rare presévérance à poursuivre un projet jusqu'à son entier accomplissement: son projet une fois conçu, il est clair

que le premier devait tomber dans les filets du second."
Voyage, pp. 266–67.

50. "Spring, which manifests itself early in that meridional latitude, gave the Kalmucks the hope of a good season." ("Le printemps qui s'annonce de bonne heure dans la patrie méridionale de ce pays, présentait aux kalmuks les avantages d'une belle saison.") *Voyage,* p. 314.

51. " 'the anarchy of dreams' presides in her philosophy [Germany]; and the restless elements of opinion, throughout every region of debate, mould themselves eternally, like the billowy sands of the desert as beheld by Bruce, into towering columns, soar upwards to a giddy altitude, then stalk about for a minute, all aglow with fiery colour, and finally unmould and 'dislimn,' with a collapse as sudden as the motions of that eddying breeze under which their vapoury architecture had arisen." "Literary Reminiscences," II, 202. See also "Dr. Samuel Parr," V, 48.

52. "Ces fugitifs . . . se précipitèrent en foule avec leurs bestiaux, sans même quitter leurs habits, et s'enfoncèrent au milieu des eaux, autant que la profondeur du lac le leur permit, pour apaiser la soif qui les dévorait si cruellement. Plusieurs furent victimes de leur imprudence; un plus grand nombre succomba sous le fer des kirghises, dans un nouveau et sanglant combat: sans moyens de se défendre, les kalmuks les plus lestes eurent à peine le temps de passer le fleuve, et de se soustraire ainsi à la poursuite de leurs ennemis." *Voyage,* pp. 334–35.

53. I owe to Professor André von Gronicka the suggestion that in this description of the massacre of the Kalmucks in Lake Tengis, De Quincey may have been echoing, consciously or unconsciously, a famous page of Greek history: Thucydides' very similar description of the slaughter of the Athenians under Nicias by the Syracusans in the river Assinarus. Thucydides writes: "The Athenians pushed on for the Assinarus, impelled by the attacks made upon them from every side by a numerous cavalry and the swarm of other arms, fancying that they should breathe more freely if once across the river, and driven on also by their exhaustion and craving for water. Once there they rushed in, and all order was at an end, each man wanting to cross first, and the attacks of the enemy making it difficult to cross at all; forced to huddle together, they fell against and trod down one another, some dying immediately upon the javelins, others getting entangled together and stumbling over the articles of baggage, without being able to rise again. Meanwhile

the opposite bank, which was steep, was lined by the Syracusans, who showered missiles down upon the Athenians, most
of them drinking greedily and heaped together in disorder in
the hollow bed of the river. The Peloponnesians also came
down and butchered them, especially those in the water, which
was thus immediately spoiled, but they went on drinking just
the same, mud and all, bloody as it was, most even fighting to
have it." *The Peloponnesian War*, tr. R. Crawley (New York,
1934), Bk. VII, 451.

54. XIII, 159–244.

55. For Masson's discussion of the source, see the "Editorial
Note." (XIII, 245–50)

56. "C'est moins un récit que la matière d'un récit; c'est un sec
et court sommaire sans animation et sans vie." *Revue des Deux
Mondes*, XVII (February, 1847), 635.

57. "Ses fautes, cependant, si graves qu'elles puissent être, n'in-
spirent pas le dégoût. C'est une nature sauvage, livrée à elle-
même, qui n'a conscience ni du bien, ni du mal. Élevée jusqu'à
quinze ans par des religieuses ignorantes, abandonnée depuis
cette époque à tous les hasards de la vie errante, à tous les in-
stincts d'une nature vulgaire, Catalina n'a pu apprendre d'autre
morale que celle des grands chemins, des camps et des matelots.
Elle ne sait évidemment pas ce qu'elle fait." *Ibid.*

58. Aristotle, *De Poetica*, tr. Ingram Bywater (London, 1942),
1451^b29.

59. "Le voyageurs étaient arrivés à un endroit où s'élèvent
comme des vagues sombres, au milieu des neiges, d'énormes
blocs de rochers. L'héroïne chercha vainement, à l'abri de ces
pierres, quelques-uns de ces buissons qui leur avaient permis
parfois d'allumer un petit foyer; toute végétation avait disparu;
à ces hauteurs, l'homme seul a droit de vivre. Alors, ne sachant
que faire ni quel parti prendre, elle imagina, pour mieux
s'orienter de grimper sur un des blocs de pierre d'où son regard
embrasserait un horizon plus étendu. Elle se hissa péniblement,
atteignit le sommet le plus élevé de ces monticules et jeta les
yeux autour d'elle. Tout à coup elle poussa un cri et courut de
nouveau vers ses campagnons. Assis et appuyé contre un rocher
voisin, un homme lui était apparu! Quel pouvait être ce
voyageur? C'était un libérateur peut-être, et sans doute il
n'était pas seul! L'annonce de ce secours inattendu rendit du
courage aux deux moribonds; ils se levèrent et suivèrent Catalina. Arrivés à vingt pas de l'endroit désigné, ils aperçurent

l'étranger, qui n'avait pas bougé de place. Il était assis, à demi caché derrière une pointe de rocher, dans la position d'un tirailleur qui guette ou d'un chasseur à l'affût.—Qui vive! cria Catalina en soulevant son arquebuse avec effort. L'étranger ne répondit pas, ne bougea pas et ne parut pas avoir entendu.—Qui vive! répéta Catalina. Cette seconde sommation fut aussi vaine que la première. Les trois voyageurs s'avancèrent lentement, avec précaution, en longeant le rocher, et arrivèrent enfin à deux pas du guetteur silencieux qui leur tournait le dos.—Eh! l'ami, dit Cataline en lui frappant sur l'épaule, dormez-vous?—Mais à peine avait-elle prononcé ces mots, qu'elle recula de trois pas en pâlissant d'épouvante. Au toucher de Catalina, l'homme assis avait roulé sur la neige comme une masse inerte. C'était un cadavre gelé, raide comme une statue; son visage était bleu et sa bouche entr'ouverte par un affreux sourire." *Revue, op. cit.*, 608–9.

60. "Vers le soir, elle crut apercevoir un arbre dans le lointain, elle revenait donc vers le pays des vivans! Elle rassembla tout ce qui restait en elle de force et d'énergie, et marcha si bien, qu'elle atteignit enfin cet arbre de salut; mais là son courage la trahit, ses jambes tremblantes fléchirent, elle s'étendit sur la terre et tomba dans un état qui participait à la fois de l'évanouissement et du sommeil. Cet engourdissement dura toute la nuit; quand elle revint à elle, le jour naissait, la température était relativement très douce, et l'air tiède l'étouffait." *Ibid.*, 609.

61. De Quincey's pride in this passage is suggested by a remark in a letter of September 19, 1847, to his daughter Florence. "M. tells me in a P.S. that you had read 'Schlosser.' By what strange fatality is it that, if I write a hurried paper, by its subject necessarily an inferior one, some friend is sure to show it to you? And no friend thought it worthwhile to show you the 'Spanish Nun's' passage across the Andes, or the 'Joan of Arc,' " Page, *op. cit.*, I, 349–50.

62. XIII, 70–124.

63. This inference is supported by a note De Quincey appended to the paper. "I am sensible that my record is far too diffuse. Feeling this at the very time of writing, I was yet unable to correct it; so little self-control was I able to exercise under the afflicting agitations and the unconquerable impatience of my nervous malady."—XIII, 124.

64. See Richard H. Byrns, "Some Unpublished Works of De Quincey," *PMLA*, LXXI (1956), 990–1003.

65. The newspapers compared with the *Times* were the *Courier*, the *Examiner*, and the *Sun*. The account in the *Edinburgh Annual Register* for 1812 was also consulted.

66. It is possible that the paper was based on long-hoarded notes; but if that were the case, one would expect the names and dates to be accurate.

67. The scene is that in which Raskolnikov listens at the door of the old pawn-broker, Alyona Ivanovna. *Crime and Punishment* is full of echoes of De Quincey. Raskolnikov carries an axe under his coat just as Williams carries a ship's mallet under his black surtout. Sonia resembles De Quincey's most famous character, Anne of Oxford Street.

68. *Times*, Wednesday, December 11, 1811.

CHAPTER IV *Miner or Minter?*

1. *Collected Writings*, XII, 5–156. The original title-page reads, "Klosterheim; or, the Masque. By the English Opium-Eater. William Blackwood, Edinburgh: and T. Cadell, Strand, London, MDCCCXXXII."

2. See Horace Ainsworth Eaton, *Thomas De Quincey: A Biography* (New York, 1936), pp. 346–47.

3. *Ibid.*, p. 334.

4. *Ibid.*, pp. 346–47.

5. "in purity of style and idiom, in which the Scholar is ever implied, and the scholarly never obtrudes itself, it reaches an excellence to which Sir W. Scott, with all the countless unaffected conversational charms and on-carryingness of his Diction, appears never to have aspired, rather than to have fallen short of." Letter from Coleridge to William Blackwood, May 26, 1832, in Mrs. Oliphant, *Annals of a Publishing House: William Blackwood and His Sons*, 3 vols. (Edinburgh, 1897), I, 419–20.

6. "As regards Klosterheim, he [De Quincey] would be much obliged to you if you would not publish it." Letter from Emily De Quincey to James T. Fields, March 8, 1856, in *De Quincey at Work: As Seen in One Hundred Thirty New and Newly Edited Letters*, ed. Willard Hallam Bonner (Buffalo, 1936), p. 32.

7. The title of Miss Murphy's book is *Banditry, Chivalry, and Terror in German Fiction. 1790–1830*, Private Edition, Distributed by the University of Chicago Libraries, Chicago, 1935.

8. XII, 234–85. First published in *Blackwood's Edinburgh Magazine*, August, 1838.

9. Letter from Emily De Quincey to Mrs. James T. Fields, March 6, 1858, in *De Quincey at Work*, p. 34.

10. "Dialogues of Three Templars on Political Economy: Chiefly in Relation to the Principles of Mr. Ricardo" (IX, 37–112). First published in *The London Magazine*, March, April and May, 1824.

11. J. R. McCulloch, *The Literature of Political Economy* (London, 1845), p. 33.

12. IX, 118–294.

13. These articles appeared in *Blackwood's Magazine* for September, October, and December, 1842.

14. "De Quincey versucht in der Form eines praktische Kommentars eine Einführung in die Abstraktionen Ricardos zu geben. Das eigene Gedankengut besteht in Anfügungen von Beispielen, in logischen Verbesserungen, in mathematischen Illustrationen, im Suchen nach klaren Ausdrücken und schärferer Herausbildung von Antithesen." Meyer, *op. cit.*, p. 31.

15. W. E. A. Axon, "The Canon of De Quincey's Writings," *Transactions of the Royal Society of Literature*, Second Series, XXXII, Pt. I (1913), 1–46.

16. Eaton, *op. cit.*, p. 355.

17. *The Complete Tales and Poems of Edgar Allan Poe* (New York, 1938), p. 339. Although Poe makes no specific reference to De Quincey, the latter was Blackwood's principal political writer during the decade 1830–40, the period Poe is writing about.

18. VIII, 42–83.

19. René Wellek, "De Quincey's Status in the History of Ideas," *PQ*, XXIII (July, 1944), 248–72.

20. *Blackwood's Edinburgh Magazine* was founded in 1817, *The London Magazine* in 1820. For information on the history of these magazines, see Mrs. Oliphant, *op. cit.* and Josephine Bauer, *The London Magazine 1820–29* (Oslo, 1953).

Alexis, Willibald. *Walladmor. Frei nach dem Englischen des Walter Scott.* 3 vols. Berlin, 1824.

————. *Erinnerungen von Willibald Alexis,* ed. Max Ewert. Berlin, 1905.

Aristotle. *De Poetica,* tr. Ingram Bywater. London, 1942.

Arndt, Ernst Moritz. *Erinnerungen aus dem Äusseren Leben.* Leipzig, 1840.

Axon, William E. A. "De Quincey and T. F. Dibden," *The Library,* 1907, 267–74.

————. "The Canon of De Quincey's Writings," *Transactions of the Royal Society of Literature,* Second Series, XXXII, Pt. 1 (1913), 1–46.

Bauer, Josephine. *The London Magazine 1820–29.* Oslo, 1953.

Baugh, Albert C., ed. *A Literary History of England,* New York, 1948.

Bellermann, Johann Joachim. *Geschichtliche Nachrichten aus dem Alterthume über Essäer und Therapeuten.* Berlin, 1821.

Bergmann, Benjamin, *Nomadische Streifereien unter den Kalmüken in den Jahren 1802 und 1803.* 2 vols. Riga, 1804.

————. *Voyage de Benjamin Bergmann chez les Kalmuks,* tr. M. Morris. Chatillon-sur-Seine, 1825.

Blackwood's Magazine. MSS. National Library of Scotland.

Bobrik, Hermann. *Geographie des Herodot.* Königsberg, 1838.

Byrns, Richard H. "Some Unpublished Works of De Quincey," *PMLA,* LXXI (1956), 990–1003.

De Quincey, Thomas. *The Collected Writings of Thomas De Quincey,* ed. David Masson. 14 vols. London, 1897.

————. *De Quincey's Writings.* 22 vols. Boston, 1851–59.

————. *Walladmor.* 2 vols. London, 1825.

————. *De Quincey at Work: As Seen in One Hundred Thirty*

New and Newly Edited Letters, ed. Willard Hallam Bonner. Buffalo, 1936.

————. *A Diary of Thomas De Quincey, 1803,* ed. Horace A. Eaton. New York, 1927.

————. *De Quincey and His Friends: Personal Recollections, Souvenirs and Anecdotes,* ed. James Hogg. London, 1895.

————. "De Quincey on French Drama," *More Books. The Bulletin of the Boston Public Library* (October, 1939).

Doering, Heinrich. *Friederich von Schiller's Leben.* Weimar, 1822.

Eaton, Horace Ainsworth. *Thomas De Quincey: A Biography.* New York, 1936.

————. "The Letters of De Quincey to Wordsworth," *ELH,* III (1936), 15–30.

Elton, Oliver. *A Survey of English Literature, 1780–1830.* 2 vols. London, 1924.

Elwin, Malcolm. *De Quincey.* London, 1935.

Essig, Erhart H. "Thomas De Quincey and Robert Pearse Gillies as Champions of German Literature and Thought" (Unpublished Ph.D. dissertation, Northwestern University, 1951).

Frye, Northrup, et al. *The English Romantic Poets and Essayists: A Review of Research and Criticism.* New York, 1957.

Gillies, R. P. *Memoirs of a Literary Veteran.* 3 vols. London, 1851.

Goethe, Johann Wolfgang. *Dichtung und Wahrheit.* Hamburg, 1956.

Gordon, Rev. James. *History of the Rebellion in Ireland in the Year 1798.* London, 1803.

Gordon, Thomas. *History of the Greek Revolution.* 2 vols. Edinburgh, 1833.

Herder, Johann Gottfried. *Ideen zur Philosophie der Geschichte der Menschheit, Herder's Werke,* ed. Prof. Dr. Theodor Matthias. 4 vols. Leipzig, n. d.

Hill, Matthew Davenport. *Plans for the Government and Liberal Instruction of Boys in large Numbers: Drawn from Experience.* London, 1822.

Jordan, John E. *Thomas De Quincey Literary Critic.* Berkeley, 1952.

Josephus. *Genuine Works of Josephus Flavius . . .* tr. William Whiston. London, 1737.

Lockhart, J. G. *Memoirs of Sir Walter Scott.* 5 vols. London, 1900.

———. *Lockhart's Literary Criticism,* ed. M. Clive Hildyard. Oxford, 1931.

McCulloch, J. R. *The Literature of Political Economy.* London, 1845.

Masson, David. *Thomas De Quincey.* London, 1881.

Meyer, Gertrud. *Das Verhältnis Thomas De Quincey's zur Nationalökonomie.* Freiburg, 1926.

Michelson, Peter. "Thomas De Quincey und die Kantische Philosphie," *Revue de Littérature Comparée,* XXXIII (1959), 356–75.

Monk, James Henry. *The Life of Richard Bentley, D.D.,* London, 1830.

Müller, Wilhelm. *Homerische Vorschule, eine Einleitung in das Studium der Ilias und Odyssee,* 2nd ed. Leipzig, 1836.

Murphy, Agnes Genevieve. *Banditry, Chivalry, and Terror in German Fiction. 1790–1830.* Distributed by the University of Chicago Libraries. Chicago, 1935.

Niebuhr, Barthold Georg. "Ueber die Geographie Herodots," *Königlich-Preussischen Akademie der Wissenschaften, Abhandlungen der historisch-philologischen Klasse,* 1812–13 (Berlin, 1816), pp. 209–24.

———. *A Dissertation on the Geography of Herodotus,* tr. from the German. Oxford, 1830.

Oliphant, M. O. W. *Annals of a Publishing House: William Blackwood and His Sons.* 3 vols. Edinburgh, 1897–98.

Page, H. A. (pseudonym for A. H. Japp). *Thomas De Quincey: His Life and Writings.* 2 vols. London, 1877.

Pashley, Robert. *Travels in Crete.* London, 1837.

Poe, Edgar Allan. *The Complete Tales and Poems of Edgar Allan Poe.* New York, 1938.

Pollitt, Charles. *De Quincey's Editorship of the Westmoreland Gazette.* Kendal, 1890.

Pope, Alexander. *The Works of Alexander Pope, Esq.,* ed. William Roscoe. 10 vols. London, 1824.

Praz, Mario. *The Hero in Eclipse in Victorian Fiction,* tr. Angus Davidson. London, 1956.

Proctor, Sigmund K. *Thomas De Quincey's Theory of Literature.* Ann Arbor, 1943.

Rennell, James. *The Geographical System of Herodotus.* London, 1830.

Robinson, Henry Crabb. *Henry Crabb Robinson on Books and Their Writers*, ed. Edith J. Morley. 3 vols. London, 1938.

Sackville-West, Edward. *Thomas De Quincey*. New Haven, 1936.

Saintsbury, George. "De Quincey," *Essays in English Literature*. 2 vols. London, 1923.

Sandhaas, Joseph A. "De Quincey's *Revolt of the Tartars* Seen in the Light of Chinese, French, German and English Source Material" (Unpublished Ph.D. dissertation, Boston University, 1946).

Scriptores Historiae Augustae, ed. David Magie. 3 vols. London, 1943.

Scriptores Historiae Augustae, Cum integris Notis Isaaci Casauboni, Cl. Salmasii and Jani Gruteri. 2 vols. Leyden, 1671.

Shakespeare, William. *The Dramatic Works of William Shakespeare*, ed. Thomas Campbell. London, 1866.

————. *The Dramatic Works of William Shakespeare*, ed. George Steevens, with a Memoir by Alexander Chalmers. Philadelphia, 1849.

Smith, Elizabeth. *Fragments in Prose and Verse by Miss Elizabeth Smith, lately deceased, with some account of Her Life and Character by H. M. Bowdler*. Bath, 1810.

Stockley, V. *German Literature as Known in England 1750–1830*. London, 1929.

Stockoe, F. W. *German Influence in the English Romantic Period*. Cambridge, 1926.

Suetonius. *De Vita Caesarum*, ed. J. C. Rolfe. 2 vols. London, 1951.

Valon, Alexis de. "Catalina de Erauso," *Revue des Deux Mondes*, XVII (February, 1847).

V. R. "De Quincey: Some Objections and Corrections," *Notes and Queries*, CCXXVI (1939), 417–18; CLXXVII (1939), 3–6, 42–45, 189–96; CLXXIX (1940), 204–7, 417–20, 433–36.

Wasianski, Ernst Anton. *Immanuel Kant in seinen letzten Lebensjahren*. Königsberg, 1804.

Wellek, René. "De Quincey's Status in the History of Ideas," *PQ*, XXIII (July, 1944), 248–72.

————. *Immanuel Kant in England 1793–1838*. Princeton, 1931.

Wells, John Edwin. "Wordsworth and De Quincey in Westmoreland Politics, 1818," *PMLA*, LV (December, 1940), 1080–1128.

Wordsworth, Dorothy, *George and Sarah Green, A Narrative by Dorothy Wordsworth*, ed. E. de Selincourt. Oxford, 1936.

Wordsworth, William and Dorothy. *Letters of William and Dorothy Wordsworth, The Middle Years*, ed. Ernest de Selincourt. Oxford, 1937.

INDEX